To my beautiful wife Rebecca – thank you for all your love and support over the years.

To Erin K. – thanks for all the help and hard work to make this book happen.

To all the men and women of the HPD – thank you for the countless hours of dedication and camaraderie.

To Marty P. from the FBI, OPD Vice/CEU and SJPD Vice Unit – thanks for showing me all the ropes.

Table of Contents

Introduction

There are thousands of law enforcement officers within the United States that are confronted with the epidemic of human trafficking. While human trafficking is not a new crime, it has recently taken center stage as a criminal enterprise that is extremely profitable with less risk to the traffickers. As criminals invent new ways to profit and exploit people, law enforcement has to adapt to these often horrific changing trends.

As an experienced cop, I've had to learn new ways to piece together the often complex parts of human trafficking cases. Albeit, by trial and error, I learned there is an untold amount of information provided by federal agencies and non-governmental organizations (NGO) to assist us in conducting comprehensive investigations that maximize our ability to recover victims and prosecute human traffickers.

To be successful, these complex investigations require a multitude of disciplines. The best piece of advice I can give to a peer is don't hesitate to reach out to other local, state, federal law enforcement agencies and non-governmental organizations (NGOs) to assist with your investigations. You'll find that sharing the work and coordinating your efforts with other agencies that have the same mission is productive and extremely rewarding.

I hope this book provides guidance for you to conduct complete and successful investigations and I wish you the best.

Ryan D. Cantrell

CHAPTER 1

WHAT IS HUMAN TRAFFICKING?

Human Trafficking may be one of the least understood crimes in the United States. Often referred to as "slavery without chains," it is a widespread and highly profitable crime, largely hidden from public view out of ignorance or denial of its existence in the United States. After drug dealing, human trafficking is tied with the illegal arms trade as the second largest criminal industry in the world, and it is the fastest-growing.

Human trafficking involves the recruitment, harboring, transportation, provision, or obtaining of a person for the purposes of forced labor or services through means of force, fraud, or coercion. Sex trafficking occurs when a commercial sex act is induced by force, fraud, or coercion, or when the person induced to perform such acts is under the age of 18. Human trafficking often involves severe violence to its victims as well as a host of other crimes including gang crime, drug and property crimes, organized criminal operations, and other violations of state, federal, and international law.

While data is not yet available to describe the full extent of human trafficking in the United States, available research indicates that a majority of law enforcement agencies in the United States have encountered some form of human trafficking or have been in contact with victims through routine work and investigations into other crimes. According to the estimate of the Department of State, roughly 800,000 people are trafficked across borders each year. If trafficking within countries is included in the total world figures, official U.S. estimates indicate that some 2 to 4 million people are trafficked annually. As many as 17,500 people are believed to be trafficked into the United States each year and some have estimated that 100,000 U.S. children are victims of trafficking within the United States.

Due to the hidden nature of the crime, perpetrators often operate unnoticed, and those who suffer are not likely to report themselves as victims of the crime of "human trafficking." Trafficking victims often do not see themselves as victims and may blame themselves for their situation. Discovery of this crime is therefore difficult because victims rarely self-report to law enforcement and the time and resources required to uncover the violations can be immense. Because of these facts, law enforcement training to recognize the signs of human trafficking and collaboration with NGOs working with victims of human trafficking is extremely important.

Examples of Human Trafficking Cases

USA

Alissa, 16, met an older man at a convenience store in Dallas and after a few dates accepted his invitation to move in with him. Soon Alissa's new "boyfriend" convinced her to be an escort for him, accompanying men on dates and having sex with them for money. He took her to an area known for street prostitution and forced her to hand over all of her earnings. He made Alissa get a tattoo of his nickname, branding her as his property, and he posted prostitution advertisements with her picture on an Internet site. He rented hotel rooms around Dallas and forced Alissa to have sex with men who responded to the ads. He kept an assault rifle in the closet of his apartment which he used to threaten Alissa and physically assaulted her on multiple occasions. The man later pled guilty to trafficking Alissa.

Honduras-USA

Maria was 15 when two well-dressed men driving a nice car approached her and two friends in a small Honduran village. They told the girls they were businessmen and offered to take them to the United States to work in a textile factory. Maria thought it was the perfect opportunity to help her single mother, who struggled to support seven children.

Upon arriving in Houston, the girls were held captive, beaten, raped, and forced to work in cantinas that doubled as brothels. Men would come to the cantina and choose a beer and a girl, sometimes as young as 12. They would pay for the beer and sit with the girl while she drank it. If they wanted to have sex with the girl, they would take her to the back and pay cash for a mattress, paper towels, and spermicidal. The captors beat the girls daily if they did not make enough money.

After six years, Maria was able to escape the cantina and return to her mother with the help of a kind American family. Her two friends remain missing.

Philippines-USA

Maria came to the United States with some 50 other Filipino nationals who were promised housing, transportation, and lucrative jobs at country clubs and hotels under the H2B guest worker program. Like the others, Maria dutifully paid the substantial recruitment fees to come to the United States. But when she arrived, she found that there was no employment secured for her. She did not work for weeks, but the recruiters seized her passport and prohibited her from leaving their house. She and other workers slept side-by-side on the floors of the kitchen, garage, and dining room. They were fed primarily chicken feet and innards. When the workers complained, the recruiters threatened to call the police or immigration services to arrest and deport them. A federal grand jury indicted the two defendants for conspiracy to hold the workers in a condition of forced labor.

Myths Associated with Human Trafficking

Myth #1:
All Prostitutes Are Willing Participants

Prostitution is the most common type of crime in which law enforcement officers will encounter victims of trafficking, however, there is a misconception that all prostitutes are willing participants, or even broader, that all sex trade participants are prostitutes. While this may be the case for some, it often times is not the case for victims of human trafficking, who are forced or coerced into the sex trade by traffickers. Victims of trafficking may be perceived as prostitutes because they often do not initially self-identify as victims. However, if you look beneath the surface of someone you initially identify as a "typical prostitute," you may find an innocent victim in need of help and protection.

Myth #2:
All Immigrants Smuggled into the United States Enter Willingly

There are significant differences between victims of human trafficking and migrants who are smuggled into the United States. Law enforcement officers may find themselves in a situation where the suspect is presumed to be an illegal alien because they don't speak the language and can't produce identification. While they may be in the country illegally, it doesn't necessarily mean they entered or chose to stay of their own free will. Some victims of human trafficking travel willingly and legally to the United States with the proper documentation. However, once they come into contact with their trafficker or "employer," their legal documents are usually taken from them, never to be seen again.

Myth #3:
Human Trafficking Is Only Prosecuted at the Federal Level

Because there are Federal laws that prosecute crimes involving the trafficking of humans, it is often assumed that all crimes of human trafficking are prosecuted at the Federal level and therefore there is no role or stake for state or local law enforcement. However, in many jurisdictions a majority of the enforcement and prosecution of these crimes are done on a local level. Although some states do not have human trafficking statutes which mimic federal laws, there are other violations which may be investigated and prosecuted at the state or local level. Suspects involved in human trafficking frequently commit other crimes such as murder, rape, kidnapping, battery, assault, criminal threats, sexual battery, and/or false imprisonment.

This myth stems from the view in the United States that human trafficking is an immigration issue and thus local law enforcement agencies see it as exclusively a federal responsibility. However, increasing concern about the exploitation and trafficking of human beings into the United States, particularly women and children, extends from rise in awareness and enforcement around the world.

The Trafficking Victims Protection Act (TVPA) of 2000 helped to clarify the definitions of human trafficking into two primary types:

a. **"...sex trafficking in which a commercial sex act is induced by force, fraud, or coercion, or in which the person induced to perform such an act has not attained 18 years of age."**

b. **"...the recruitment, harboring, transportation, provision, or obtaining of a person for labor or services, through the use of force, fraud, or coercion for the purpose of subjection to involuntary servitude, peonage, debt bondage, or slavery."**

Because the approximately 70 percent of internationally trafficked women end up in the sex trade, the effect of TVPA is to define such women as crime victims instead of as criminals. Whether forced into prostitution or manual labor, the exploitation of these victims continues after their entry into the United States either at the hands of those who trafficked them or sold or traded to others who profit from commercial sex or forced labor. Much of these traffickers crimes occur in the United States and can be successfully investigated and prosecuted locally.

Related Issues

Sexual exploitation and forced labor are only two of a number of problems that are associated with, or are examples of, human trafficking. Other related law enforcement concerns include:

- Trafficking in children
- The sales of babies and illegal adoptions
- Kidnapping of children
- Child pornography
- International sex tourism
- Trading in organs or body parts
- Smuggling of immigrants
- Illegal employment of aliens
- Identity theft
- Document forgery
- Domestic abuse of mail order brides
- Domestic trafficking of women and juveniles

In October 2000, Congress passed the Victims of Trafficking and Violence Protection Act of 2000 ("VTVPA"). The VTVPA is a comprehensive statute that addresses the recurring and significant problem of trafficking of persons for the purpose of committing commercial sex acts, or to subject them to involuntary servitude, peonage, debt bondage, or slavery. It is also designed to increase the protection available to victims of trafficking and other types of violent crimes. It is an attempt to address these issues on a national and international level, and affects many government and non-government agencies and organizations.

According to the "Trafficking Victims Protection Act of 2000," severe forms of trafficking in persons always include the recruitment, harboring, transportation, provision, or obtaining of a person for one of the three following purposes:

1. Labor or services, through the use of force, fraud or coercion, AND resulting in involuntary servitude, peonage, debt bondage, or slavery; OR
2. Commercial sex act, through the use of force, fraud or coercion; OR
3. If the person is under 18 years of age, any commercial sex act, whether or not force, fraud or coercion is involved.

The "Trafficking Victims Protection Act of 2000" also provides tools to combat trafficking in persons both worldwide and domestically. The Act recognizes the need to protect the victims while gaining their cooperation by providing a safe haven. Section 107(c) (3) reads: "Authority to Permit Continued Presence in the United States. Federal law enforcement officials may permit an alien individual's continued presence in the United States, if after an assessment, it is determined that such individual is a victim of a severe form of trafficking and a potential witness to such trafficking, in order to effectuate prosecution of those responsible, and such officials in investigating and prosecuting traffickers shall protect the safety of trafficking victims, including taking measures to protect trafficked persons and their family members from intimidation, threats of reprisals, and reprisals from traffickers and their associates."

Sex Trafficking

There are primarily two types of human trafficking: Sex Trafficking and Labor Trafficking. About 8 in 10 of suspected incidents of human trafficking are classified as sex trafficking, and about 1 in 10 incidents are classified as labor trafficking. Sex trafficking operations occur in highly visible venues such as street prostitution, as well as more underground locations such as closed-brothel systems that operate out of residential homes. Sex trafficking also takes place in a variety of public and private locations such as massage parlors, spas, escort services and other fronts for prostitution. This may also include other forms of sexualized labor such as stripping, exotic dancing, and semi-nude performances. Victims may start off dancing or stripping in clubs and are often coerced into more exploitative situations involving prostitution and pornography. According to a published study by the Bureau of Justice Statistics identified sex trafficking victims were more likely to be white (26%) or black (40%). Four-fifths of victims in confirmed sex trafficking incidents were identified as U.S. citizens (83%).

Drugs and alcohol play major roles in the subjugation of trafficking victims, and in sex trafficking they are a nearly universally present. Traffickers sometimes prey on women and children with pre-existing addictions, but recruiters, particularly in the transnational trade, may prefer healthier, more attractive victims and instead introduce drugs later, as they tighten their grip on victims. Both giving drugs and withholding drugs are effective and commonly used means of maintaining control over victims. Drugs and alcohol also act as a form of anesthesia, dulling physical and psychic pain, making victims capable of enduring the conditions of their servitude and thus continuing to produce profits.

Violence is at the root of "traffickers" power over victims. It is typically physical, brutal, and instructional. In the transit and indoctrination stages, violence may be used to convince victims that their survival depends on submission to their traffickers' demands. Later physical violence serves as punishment, reminds victims that they live in captivity, and acts as a means of keeping victims on edge so that they are more easily controlled. Many kinds of violence are employed. One study of victims trafficked internationally for sex and domestic servitude reported that victims were "hit, kicked, punched, struck with objects, burned, cut with knives." Rape is common and in the most extreme cases, victims are murdered. Once traffickers establish their capacity for violence, they can exercise control through threats, implicit or explicit. Traffickers threaten not only victims but also their friends and families. These threats are plausible. Traffickers often know victim's families and victims often report having seen, or knowing about, trafficker's violence, including murder, perpetrated against other victims.

Debt is another commonly used method to maintain control over trafficking victims. In one study of women recruited in the Philippines all of the victims stated they had willingly agreed to be transported to the destination county with some even paying their travel expenses in advance. However, all of the victims fell into heavy debt and became entrapped in exploitative sex trafficking.

Prostitution and Pimps

Victim identification starts with the awareness that human trafficking is often a form of gender-based violence.

Although men and boys are also subjected to sex and labor trafficking, most victims of human trafficking are female, and of these, the majority is trafficked into prostitution or a related form of commercial sexual exploitation. Due to its ubiquity, commercial sexual exploitation should be recognized as a hallmark of trafficking. The majority of people engaged in prostitution is children or were originally prostituted as children. Experts estimate that the average age of entry into prostitution for females is twelve to fourteen. Anyone prostituted as a child is by definition a trafficking victim under the federal anti-trafficking law. Since most adults in prostitution were initially prostituted as children (age seventeen or younger) and since prostituted children are necessarily victims of trafficking, one could reasonably conclude that the majority of prostituted adults have been subjected to sex trafficking at some point in their lives.

Furthermore, studies have found that the majority of women in prostitution are, at some point, under the control of a pimp. If the prostituted person is or has been under the control of a pimp or someone functioning as a pimp, she or he is likely to have been subjected to force, fraud, or coercion. Pimps are usually simultaneously intimate partners and sex traffickers. Pimps almost invariably start out by entering into sexual relationships with their victims and then use acts of sexual and physical abuse, promises of protection, devotion, and love to control the victim... After they establish their dominance, they "turn out" their victims into prostitution, exploiting them in order to reap large sums of money that support the pimp's often opulent lifestyle.

Pimps "season" their victims into submission by altering their identities, changing their names, isolating them from family and friends, persuading them that they now exist outside of mainstream society, and subjecting them to a brutal and rigid regimen of power and control. Victims are routinely called gender-based slurs like "bitch" and "whore," are required to behave in a servile and deferential manner, often by referring to their pimps by terms like "Daddy," and are brutally punished for the slightest infraction of their pimp's rules. Reducing the women and girls they prostitute to the condition of chattel slaves, some pimps literally mark them as their property by branding them with tattoos that display the pimp's name, pornographic imagery, the victim's pimp-assigned moniker, or demeaning slogans like "Daddy's li'l bitch."

Although little is known about the prostitution of boys and young men, experts increasingly are finding high levels of gender-based violence and exploitation in their histories, which should raise a similar presumption that they are likely to be victims of sex trafficking.

Given these links between the sexual exploitation of children, pimps and prostitution learning that a woman is involved in prostitution should create a presumption that she is a trafficking victim. Law enforcement officers who come into contact with prostituted women should be on high alert that there is a substantial likelihood that they are dealing with a victim of sex trafficking.

Servile Marriage or "Mail Order Brides"

While the practice of arranging to marry someone from another country is not necessarily trafficking, some traffickers hide their operations by posing as international marriage brokerage services. The United States is the primary importer of mails order brides and the main source country is the Philippines. Other target countries include Russia where "marriage agencies" provide a catalog of available woman and subsequently hold "mixers" to which U.S. men travel and attend. The women are charged a substantial fee for inclusion in the catalog and attendance at the social events, often times consuming their and their families combined savings.

The precise extent to which traffickers exploit the mail order bride industry is not known, however, it can be an ideal front for their business. Traffickers find mail order bride services and marriage agencies attractive because they are largely unregulated and permitted to recruit women openly.

The determining factors for trafficking are the circumstances the "bride" faces once in the United States;

27

is she being held in a condition of servitude through the use of force, fraud, or coercion for the purposes of forced labor or commercial sexual exploitation? Situations of servile marriage create inherent vulnerabilities, so it is important to ask additional questions to try to understand the individual's welfare and freedom.

Labor Trafficking

Labor traffickers use force, fraud or coercion to recruit, harbor, transport, obtain or employ a person for labor or services in involuntary servitude, peonage, debt bondage or slavery. Forced labor occurs in various forms including domestic servitude such as nannies and maids, sweatshop factories, janitorial jobs, construction sites, farm work, restaurants and panhandling. According to a published study by the Bureau of Justice Statistics labor trafficking victims, who were more likely to be Hispanic (63%) or Asian (17%).Most confirmed labor trafficking victims were identified as undocumented aliens (67%) or qualified aliens (28%).

Most instances of forced labor occur as unscrupulous employers take advantage of gaps in law enforcement to exploit vulnerable workers. These workers are made more vulnerable to forced labor practices because of unemployment, poverty, crime, discrimination, corruption, political conflict, and cultural acceptance of the practice. Immigrants are particularly vulnerable, but individuals are also forced into labor in their own countries. Female victims of forced or bonded labor, especially women and girls in domestic servitude, are often sexually abused.

Forced labor is a form of human trafficking that can be harder to identify and estimate than sex trafficking. It may not involve the same criminal networks profiting from transnational trafficking for sexual exploitation. More often, individuals are guilty of subjecting one domestic servant or hundreds of unpaid workers at a factory to involuntary servitude.

Bonded Labor

One form of force or coercion is the use of a bond, or debt, to keep a person under subjugation. This is referred to in law and policy as "bonded labor" or "debt bondage." It is criminalized under U.S. law and included as a form of exploitation related to trafficking in the United Nations Protocol To Prevent, Suppress, and Punish Trafficking in Persons, Especially Women and Children (UN TIP Protocol). Many workers around the world fall victim to debt bondage when traffickers or recruiters unlawfully exploit an initial debt the worker assumed as part of the terms of employment or when workers inherit debt in more traditional systems of bonded labor. Traditional bonded labor in South Asia enslaves huge numbers of people from generation to generation.

Involuntary Servitude

People become trapped in involuntary servitude when they believe an attempted escape from their situation would result in serious physical harm to them or others, or when they are kept in a condition of servitude through the abuse or threatened abuse of the legal processes. Victims are often economic migrants and low-skilled laborers who are trafficked from less developed communities to more prosperous and developed places. Many victims are physically and verbally abused, experience breach of an employment contract, and/or are held captive (or perceive themselves as held captive).

Debt Bondage and Involuntary Servitude among Guest Workers

The vulnerability of migrant laborers to trafficking schemes is especially disturbing because this population is so sizeable in some regions. Three potential contributors can be discerned: 1) Abuse of contracts; 2) Inadequate local laws governing the recruitment and employment of migrant laborers; and 3) The intentional imposition of exploitative and often illegal costs and debts on these laborers in the source country or state, often with the complicity and/or support of labor agencies and employers in the destination country or state.

Some abuses of contracts and difficult conditions of employment do not in themselves constitute involuntary servitude, though use or threat of physical force or restraint to compel a worker to enter into or continue labor or service may convert a situation into one of forced labor. Costs imposed on laborers for the "privilege" of working abroad can place laborers in a situation highly vulnerable to debt bondage. However, these costs alone do not constitute debt bondage or involuntary servitude. When combined with exploitation by unscrupulous labor agents or employers in the destination country, these costs or debts, when excessive, can become a form of debt bondage.

Involuntary Domestic Servitude

Domestic workers may be trapped in servitude through the use of force or coercion, such as physical (including sexual) or emotional abuse. Children are particularly vulnerable. Domestic servitude is particularly difficult to detect because it occurs in private homes, which are often unregulated by public authorities. For example, there is great demand in some wealthier countries of Asia and the Middle East for domestic servants who sometimes fall victim to conditions of involuntary servitude.

Forced Child Labor

Most international organizations and national laws indicate that children may legally engage in light work. In contrast, the worst forms of child labor are being targeted for eradication by nations across the globe. The sale and trafficking of children and their entrapment in bonded and forced labor are clearly the worst forms of child labor. Any child who is subject to involuntary servitude, debt bondage, peonage or slavery through the use of force, fraud or coercion is a victim of trafficking in persons regardless of the location of that exploitation.

Examples of Incidents Which May Involve Human Trafficking

- Prostitution investigations and/or sting operations involving foreign nationals or younger prostitutes
- Investigations involving the operation of common prostitution fronts such as massage parlors and strip clubs
- Domestic abuse incidents
- A person, particularly a foreign national or minor, with unexplained physical injury or abuse
- "False" or "accidental" 911 calls
- Encounters with migrant workers where a foreman or supervisor attempts to keep the group away from the law enforcement officers or attempts to control all communication between the officer and the group
- Fights between people in which money is owed
- Crimes involving immigrant children in situations such as prostitution or forced labor
- Crimes or welfare checks involving children where there are no guardians present

- Adult and child pornography
- Drugs and weapons trafficking where the suspect may have been used as an "expendable" courier
- Kidnapping
- Money laundering
- Organized crime
- Shoplifting or organized retail theft
- Routine traffic violations
- Workplace disputes

If any of these indicators are present, further inquiry should be made to determine if there is a situation of human trafficking.

Human Trafficking Vs. Smuggling

There are key differences between the crimes of human trafficking and human smuggling. Smuggling occurs when someone is paid to assist another in the illegal crossing of borders. This relationship typically ends after the border has been crossed and the individual has paid the smuggler a fee for assistance. If the smuggler sells or "brokers" the smuggled individual into a condition of servitude, or if the smuggled individual cannot pay the smuggler and is then forced to work that debt off, the crime has now turned from smuggling into human trafficking. The key distinction between trafficking and smuggling lies in the individual's freedom of choice. A person may choose and arrange to be smuggled into a country, but when a person is forced into a situation of exploitation where their freedom is taken away, they are a victim of human trafficking.

Human Smuggling

Human smuggling is the facilitation, transportation, attempted transportation or illegal entry of a person(s) across an international border, in violation of one or more countries laws, either clandestinely or through deception, such as the use of fraudulent documents. Often, human smuggling is conducted in order to obtain a financial or other material benefit for the smuggler, although financial gain or material benefit are not necessarily elements of the crime. For instance, sometimes people engage in smuggling to reunite their families. Human smuggling is generally with the consent of the person(s) being smuggled, who often pay large sums of money. The vast majority of people who are assisted in illegally entering the United States are smuggled, rather than trafficked.

Smuggled persons may become victims of other crimes. In addition to being subjected to unsafe conditions on the smuggling journeys, smuggled aliens may be subjected to physical and sexual violence. Frequently, at the end of the journey, smuggled aliens are held hostage until their debt is paid off by family members or others. It is also possible that a person being smuggled may at any point become a trafficking victim.

The Immigration and Nationalization Act, Section 274(a)(1), (2), provides for criminal penalties under Title 8, United States Code, Section 1324, for acts or attempts to bring unauthorized aliens to or into the United States, transport them within the U.S., harbor unlawful aliens, encourage entry of illegal aliens, or conspire to commit these violations, knowingly or in reckless disregard of illegal status.

Human Trafficking

Unlike smuggling, which is often a criminal commercial transaction between two willing parties who go their separate ways once their business is complete, trafficking specifically targets the trafficked person as an object of criminal exploitation. The purpose from the beginning of the trafficking enterprise is to profit from the exploitation of the victim. It follows that fraud, force or coercion all plays a major role in trafficking.

It may be difficult to make a determination between smuggling and trafficking in the initial phase. Trafficking often includes an element of smuggling, specifically, the illegal crossing of a border. In some cases the victim may believe they are being smuggled, but are really being trafficked, as they are unaware of their fate. For example, there have been cases where women trafficked for sexual exploitation may have knowingly agreed to work in the sex industry and believed that they would have decent conditions and be paid a decent wage. What they did not realize is that the traffickers would take most or all of their income, keep them in bondage and subject them to physical force or sexual violence. The victims may also have believed they were being smuggled into the United States where they would be given a job as a nanny or model, later realizing that the so-called smugglers deceived them and that they would be forced to work in the sex industry.

Conversely, persons being smuggled may sometimes willingly enter into "contracts" with the smugglers to work off a smuggling debt. Unless the aliens' labor or services are enforced through the forms of coercion set forth in the trafficking statutes, such deferred repayment does not make these people trafficking victims. However, a work-based debt can be an "indicator" of trafficking, and such a situation could trigger further examination to determine whether the aliens are victims of trafficking or extortion.

Human trafficking does not require the crossing of an international border — it does not even require the transportation of victims from one locale to another. Victims of severe forms of trafficking are not all illegal aliens; they may, in fact, be U.S. citizens, legal residents, or visitors. Victims do not have to be women or children — they may also be adult males.

While trafficking victims are often found in sweatshops, domestic work, restaurant work, agricultural labor, prostitution and sex entertainment, they may be found anywhere in the U.S. doing almost anything profitable to their handlers. Because victims may not recognize that they have been victimized, or may be forced into protecting their exploiters self-proclamation of their status is not required.

Traffickers

Traffickers include recruiters, transporters, exploiters, and others who enable or participate in the trade and exploitation of other people. Criminals engaged in human trafficking range from amateur family-run organizations to sophisticated transnational organized crime syndicates. Certain aspects of trafficking in Europe, for example, are largely supported by Russian and Albanian gangs and by the Italian mafia, whereas trafficking in Asia is largely controlled by Chinese criminal groups and the Japanese Yakuza. These international groups increasingly interact with local networks to provide transportation, safe houses, local contacts, and documentation. They are often aided by corrupt police and migration officials.

Female traffickers reportedly play a more prominent role in human trafficking than in other international crimes. Their role may vary, ranging from managing and controlling operations to helping or assisting male traffickers with certain aspects of the crime, such as victim recruitment. In some cases, female traffickers were once victims themselves.

Traffickers acquire their victims in several ways, but the primary method involves recruitment via a personal or familial contact. Sometimes women are kidnapped outright in one country and taken forcibly to another. In other cases, traffickers entice victims to migrate voluntarily with false promises of well-paying jobs or through false opportunities to study or travel abroad. In some cases, traffickers approach individuals or their families, often through informal networks of families and friends, directly with offers of lucrative jobs elsewhere. Russian crime gangs, for example, reportedly use marriage agency databases and matchmaking parties to find victims. After providing transportation and false documents to get victims to their destination, they subsequently charge exorbitant fees for those services, often creating lifetime debt bondage. In the case of trafficked children, traffickers may simply purchase them from their guardians.

STAGE 1
Recruitment

STRATEGIES	TECHNIQUES
▪ Select vulnerable women—usually poor, young, and uneducated—who are easy to trick and will believe promises of future employment ▪ Hide behind an apparently legal business, such as an employment or travel agency ▪ Get victim into debt or find a debt-ridden family ▪ Traffic from countries that benefit from foreign exchange resulting from export of trafficked women ▪ Offer services as "coyote" or smuggler	▪ False promises of work and well paying jobs ▪ False promises of work visas and passports ▪ Offer of safe passage to destination country ▪ Use person from victim's culture to recruit ▪ Use of tourist visas without work visas ▪ Recruiter buys young girl for small sum ▪ Arrange marriage to American men including serviceman ▪ Advertise for women needed for "housekeeping" work ▪ Kidnapping ▪ Trafficker convinces the woman he loves her ▪ Pay for client travel, give loan

STAGE 2
Transportation and Entry

STRATEGIES	TECHNIQUES
■ Provide a service such as all necessary documentation and travel arrangements ■ Use a tourist or employment agency as a front ■ Provide guide service ■ Search for weak points of entry into the United States	■ Document forgery ■ Stolen passports and visas ■ Bribery of border officials ■ Transportation in concealed vehicles ■ Provide recruits with tourist visas ■ Employers manipulate special visas Handlers (e.g. "coyotes" on Mexico/U.S. border) guide individuals across borders or over difficult terrain, sometimes providing transportation

STAGE 3
Delivery and Marketing

STRATEGIES	TECHNIQUES
▪ Make contact with clients using standard marketing techniques	▪ Advertising in pornographic magazines and websites and in the ethnic media
▪ Prearrange deals through legal or illegal businesses, such as domestic employment agencies, entertainment agencies, and escort services	▪ Establish matchmaking websites to advertise women
▪ Market through organized crime rings for sex trade	▪ Deliver to farm labor, sweat shops; domestic service agencies etc.
▪ Keep trafficked woman dependent on trafficker until delivery	▪ Mail order brides and matchmaking camps
	▪ Retention or confiscation of travel documents
	Traffic women domestically by constantly moving them between cities and states to satisfy demand for new women and to keep the women isolated

STAGE 4
Exploitation

STRATEGIES	TECHNIQUES
<ul><li>Exploit alien status</li><li>Threaten violence against woman's relatives in home country</li><li>Use actual violence to ensure compliance and silence</li><li>Create and maintain debt</li><li>Create and maintain alcohol and drug dependency</li><li>Exploit ambiguities in and lax enforcement of sex trade laws</li><li>Keep in isolation</li></ul>	<ul><li>Retention of passports and visas</li><li>Threaten to turn over to authorities</li><li>Keep imprisoned in the place of employment</li><li>Sex trade: forced prostitution, off street prostitution, night clubs, exotic dancing, escort services</li><li>Forced labor: bonded labor, virtual imprisonment, indentured labor, coercion and violence; labor intensive manufacturing (e.g. clothing trade) or rural farm labor</li><li>Massage parlors, nail salons, employment agencies as fronts for illegal activity Move from place to place</li></ul>

CHAPTER 2

CONTROL METHODS IN HUMAN TRAFFICKING

Success for traffickers only comes if they can control their victims. By definition, a victim of human trafficking does not consent to what is happening to them. Even though in some cases it may appear the victim consents, closer examination reveals that their consent was invalidated through the use of force, fraud, coercion, deception, or other means.

Victim control is maintained in a number of ways. These methods include:

- Violence and threats of violence

- Deception

- Imprisonment

- Collusion

- Debt bondage

- Relationship Control
- Isolation

- Exploitation of religion, culture and beliefs

While any single method may be used, most traffickers use a blend of control measures. This blend will vary according to the individual victim, the state of the trafficking process, the success of past techniques on the part of the trafficker, and the location of the victim (in their country of origin or the United States). It is important to remember that the absence of physical injury or a history of assault does not mean the victim is not being controlled via other means.

Deception is commonly used in the recruiting process to obtain victims. Promises of employment, higher wages, and expanded opportunities which might not exist in their home country are frequent enticements. Deception might be blended with collusion and debt bondage-compromising the victim into believing they are indebted to the trafficker for legal or financial obligations. For instance a trafficker might tell the victim they had to bribe a government employee to get work permits or travel documents or travel fees were paid for in advance of the victim's future earnings.

As the trafficking progresses though the stages, some control measures will lose their efficiency or the traffickers may change their approach. Once arriving at their destination it may no longer be possible to deceive a victim into believing the initial recruitment promises. Control often escalates into more threatening or violent means. Debts incurred by the victim may increase over time due to added expenses or "interest."

Some traffickers may make small concession to help maintain control over the victim and reduce their attempts to escape. Small gifts, limited privileges, allowing the victim to spend or keep some of their own money, or brief moments of freedom are common tactics which cause the victim to believe they are advancing their situation when in reality they are still firmly under the trafficker's control. These concessions are commonly combined with subtle or overt threats of violence in a "carrot and stick" approach.

How to Deal with a Trafficker's Control Methods

Violence and threats of violence

Violence or threats may be used at any stage of the trafficking process in order to establish or maintain control over the victim. The victim, their friends and/or relatives may the subjected to or targets of threats and violence.

Physical violence in the early stages of the human trafficking process may vary depending on local conditions, the location of the victim and the trafficker, and the type of trafficking involved-forced labor or sexual exploitation. In sexual exploitation cases, victims may initially be recruited through deception and violence. Threats and violence materialize later in the process as the trafficker attempts to achieve the victim's compliance.

Victims do not necessarily need to be directly threatened to live in tremendous fear of violence. The simple suggestion by a trafficker that he or she knows the victim's family and/or where they live may be enough to scare a person into compliance. Other common methods of indirect threats include telling stories of what happened to prior non-compliant victims or by making an example out of a victim who attempts to escape or deigns to become non-compliant.

It is important to remember international human traffickers may have a long reach in their ability to inflict injury on a victim's in their home country. The victim may be aware or believe a criminal organization has members or associates in the region their family lives. The victim may also know or believe the traffickers have connections with corrupt government officials, including law enforcement, in their home country. The traffickers may only imply a threat, but what is important is that the victim believes it can be carried out, not whether it actually could.

Dealing with Violence and Threats

Violence against victims of trafficking at the hands of the criminals may be obvious, but in many cases can be subtle or concealed. Do not assume a victim has not been subjected to violence simply because they do not have visible injuries or fail to initially report past assaults. Victims may not initially be willing to admit they have been assaulted because of fear, threats, or the social or cultural stigmas which may be associated with victims of sexual assault. In some countries in the world it is still common the blame the victim, irrespective of the circumstances.

While interviewing a victim it is not always prudent to initially introduce the topic of violence. Victims may choose not to divulge physical assaults until later in the investigations. However, law enforcement officers should still look for objective indicators of assault including indications of severe emotional trauma, accounts of assault told by other victims, and suspect statements regarding the use of violence to maintain control.

Look for signs of injuries during the initial encounter with a suspected trafficking victim and document those injuries as soon as possible. Injuries which can only be seen by without removing clothes should be done by a medical professional as appropriate.

Deception Control

Many human trafficking cases start with the victim being deceived by a recruiter or other member of the trafficking organization. This may be complete deception such a when a victim is told they will be working in a bar and are subsequently forced into prostitution. Deception may be partial such as when a victim is recruited to work as a domestic servant, but are denied wages and kept in slave-like conditions.

Deception is usually used in the early stages of the trafficking process. Usually, the victim either realizes the truth or is told by the criminals that they have been trafficked. Once the deception is revealed the trafficker may have to rely on a different control mechanism, or combination of control mechanisms such as violence and/or isolation.

In some source countries, deception as a control tactics may be commonly used. These include countries where there is substantial migration. In these situations, potential victims may know or have heard of others who have successfully migrated, even if the migration was illegal. The potential victims are usually aware of remittances sent back to their families by legal or illegal immigrants. Some traffickers allow their victims to send small remittances back to their families in order to make them more compliant and to allay the families suspicions back home.

The victim's expectations in their home country can make it particularly easy for traffickers to use deceptive techniques to recruit them. People in developing countries commonly have unrealistic expectation of what life is like in the United States and are receptive to stories about how good life is in this country compared to theirs. Victims may also be disinclined to believe negative stories they have heard regarding the trafficking network in anticipation of a better life for themselves and their families.

Traffickers may attempt to instill fear in their victims of U.S. government officials and law enforcement by suggesting corruption exists at all levels. Victims may be told they are subject to arrest, prosecution, and deportation if they are discovered or go to the authorities. Victims may have a factual basis to believe this based on their own experiences in their home country. They may have seen or experienced corruption by officials in their native land. In some cases the victim may be aware of friends or family who have been prosecuted for illegal entry and subsequently deported.

Dealing with Deception Control

Be aware of signs the victim may have been recruited or controlled through deceptive means. Examples include evidence such as advertisements which offer jobs in the United States in unrealistic occupations or inflated wages. Recover any advertisements or other evidence such as letters which may show traffickers have attempted to recruit victims through deceptive means.

Responses during the interview of the victim may indicate deception was used to either recruit or maintain control over the victim. Victims should be questioned about the deceptive means and methods the traffickers used to recruit or control them. Be mindful the victim may feel embarrassed or ashamed they were duped. Try to avoid judgmental questions which could make the victim defensive such as "Didn't you think it was suspicious?" or "Did you really believe…?"

Evidence or intelligence about deceptive recruiting techniques should be shared with other law enforcement agencies, particularly federal law enforcement. Many traffickers use the same established recruitment techniques frequently and sharing any intelligence regarding sources and methods may help identify other victims, as well as, components of the larger trafficking network.

Imprisonment Control

Traffickers may use direct imprisonment or something very similar to imprisonment, as a method of control. Again, this may vary according to the form of trafficking, the location and the stage in the trafficking process.

Examples of imprisonment that have been seen include brothels where victims were held in locked buildings, agricultural workers kept in secure compounds under guard and domestic servants who are not allowed to leave houses.

Even where a person may appear to have been given some liberty this may be an illusion. There have been cases where victims are only allowed out under the close supervision of a "guard."

Dealing with Imprisonment Control

"Indicators of trafficking in persons" gives more detailed suggestions about what might indicate imprisonment is involved in a trafficking case. These include:

- Fences designed to prevent people from leaving premises;
- Locks on the outside of doors;
- Guards that prevent people from leaving premises;
- People living at places that would normally only be work places;
- Evidence of any form of personal physical restraint such as handcuffs, rope and/or tape;
- Evidence of "guards" and escorts at all times.

Look for this type of evidence on visits to premises whether they are routine or specifically intended to be anti-human trafficking operations.

Brief law enforcement and other agencies, such as health and safety and fire inspectors on what to look for on routine visits to premises that might indicate imprisonment.

Plan interviews to identify if imprisonment exists in your investigation. Use the indicators above to help plan the interview.

Collusion Control

Victims are likely to be easier to control if the traffickers involve them in colluding with what they are being forced to do. For instance, traffickers involved in sexual exploitation may give victims a little money. Accepting the money can have the psychological impact on the victim of making them feel they are getting benefit from their exploitation making them "guilty." The victim may accept the money because they feel it gives them some benefit at least from their exploitation and it may allow them to support their families.

Victims who have been partially deceived may be particularly vulnerable to collusion control. A woman who knew she was going to work as a prostitute may feel she can do nothing about the fact she did not consent to sex every time, or without a condom and/or to a certain sexual act.

Collusion in criminal acts frequently features in trafficking cases. Where a person is trafficked across international borders, they may have entered a state illegally or entered legally, but broken immigration laws by overstaying or working outside the terms of their visa.

Victims of trafficking in persons may have committed acts that are illegal, e.g., pick pocketing, theft, credit card and check fraud or transport of drugs. Victims may have committed acts that are illegal in some jurisdictions: begging, prostitution, or some form of it. Such acts may not be illegal in the destination state, but they may be illegal in their country of origin or vice versa.

Trafficking victims may have taken illegal drugs for a number of reasons: when administered by traffickers, to "escape" from their situation or because they were addicted before they were trafficked.

Anyone who has committed a crime (or believes what they have done is a crime) is vulnerable to blackmail to ensure his or her compliance.

"Promotion" to membership has been seen in a number of cases, particularly those involving sexual exploitation. People who were originally trafficked may be come recruiters, escorts or may act as enforcers, "maids" or "kitchen mamas" in brothels. Collusion of this type is complex in its origins and difficult to investigate. On one hand, law enforcement agencies are faced with a person at the heart of the trafficking, on the other a possible victim who has been exploited.

Dealing with Collusion Control

Find out what your domestic policy is on non-prosecution or non-punishment of offences committed by victims of trafficking. Offences committed in the process of being trafficked, such as illegal entry to a country, may be exempt from prosecution in some circumstances. Establish what processes you need to follow to allow non-liability.

Where collusion control is present, other forms of control may have been applied prior to collusion such as deception, violence or imprisonment. Look for any evidence that other forms of control may have been used. Use both witness and suspect interviews to help obtain such evidence.

Never make promises you cannot keep to people you suspect may have been controlled through collusion.

If you suspect collusion, probe precise details of what, how, when and where it happened, and who was involved. Both witness and suspect interviews may reveal information that leads you to suspect collusion.

Corroborate what you are being told as much as you can.

Consider using expert witnesses in court if allowed in your jurisdiction. Psychologists may be able to explain to a court how the processes of collusion work.

Discuss with prosecutors when deciding how to deal with a person you suspect may have been controlled through collusion.

Debt Bondage Control

Debt bondage involves charging fees to victims for transport, accommodations, food and a range of other "expenses" that have allegedly been incurred by the traffickers. These expenses are often completely fictitious or greatly exaggerated.

Interest charged on the "debt" is frequently very high and further charges are often added to the bill, for example rent on rooms in brothels or deductions for costs of living for domestic servants. Fines may be imposed for a range of "offences" that are devised by the traffickers.

It is often impossible for the victim to pay off the debt due to the combination of high interest rates and constant additions to what are "owed."

Victims may be told that they will only have to pay for their travel, etc., when they are working but are not told how much this will be or what they will have to do to earn the money. In some cases the victim may pay cash up front believing they are to be smuggled, only to be asked for more money enroute; there belief is that they have been trafficked and the "debt" will be used to control and exploit them.

In some cases victims have been able to pay-off a debt bond. In such cases, traffickers may need to remove the victim as she or he presents independent competition to their operations. In other cases, such victims may be promoted and become part of the trafficking network.

Relationship Control

Victims may consider themselves to be in a relationship with one or more of their traffickers. Commonly seen examples include parents, family and boyfriend-girlfriend relationships and what is sometimes known as "Stockholm syndrome" where victims associate themselves with their captors and exploiters.

Relationship control may use a blend or other methods such as violence, deception, collusion and taking oaths.

Parents and others with control over children have been found to be involved in child trafficking in many cases. Examples include 'selling" children for labor or sexual exploitation, forced begging or domestic servitude. The control is often simply that the child trusts the parent or other relative or may have no choice in the matter.

Boyfriend-girlfriend relationships are seen in many cases of trafficking for sexual exploitation. This can range from a man who moves his girlfriend around for his friends to have sex with, to a person who targets a woman, forms a relationship and then deceives her into moving to another country.

Emotional control may be used where women are asked to "prove" their love by doing something they would not normally consent to. Victims are promised love, safety, marriage, family, housing and general stability by their traffickers. Victims want to believe their traffickers will provide these things, particularly given the unstable backgrounds of many victims. Victims may also be drawn in to complicity in drug use or transport or asked to sell sex to support a man's drug habit. Violence has been seen where "boyfriends" assault or threaten women to ensure compliance. Oaths and promises are common in relationships in some countries; this is exploited by traffickers in ways explained in more detail below.

Control within relationships between men and women for the purposes of trafficking in persons often have much in common with some forms of domestic abuse and can mirror attitudes within a society of acceptable behavior between the genders or their respective roles. Victims may be vulnerable to this type of control if they have been in abusive relationships in the past.

Dealing with Relationship Control

Remember that people in relationships with victims of trafficking may be involved in their exploitation. Be wary about informing them the victim is with you or using them as social supporters in interviews.

Do not return victims to relationships without assessing whether the people in that relationship were involved in the trafficking process. Assess possible risks to victims even where the person was not previously involved in trafficking: for example, if an uncle lives in extreme poverty, will he take the same opportunity to sell a child victim as the father did?

Victims should receive counseling as soon as it is possible to help them break a potential cycle of abuse in their lives. Only trained counselors should be used, and special care must be taken, especially with child victims. Any decision must aim at the best interests of the child; specialized counselors can also help when making these decisions.

Isolation Control

Victims of trafficking are likely to be isolated by the nature of their circumstances, away from their homes and family, often not speaking the local language, lacking money and with restrictions on their movement. Traffickers may use a number of other methods to increase this sense of isolation.

Access to communications equipment such as phones is likely to be restricted. The constant presence of traffickers and their associates also mean it may be difficult to write and post letters.

Social life may be non-existent or very limited. Not allowing access to religious services has an impact on people of faith that is explored below but it also has the effect of eliminating an opportunity to socialize.

Locations where victims of trafficking are held may be remote and difficult to access. This applies particularly in cases of agricultural, mining and quarrying exploitation.

Domestic servitude cases often involve a single trafficking victim in a household. Naturally isolating as this situation is, loneliness may be increased by control measures such as making the victim eat meals alone and not giving any days off.

Dealing with Isolation Control

Look for signs of isolation control when visiting premises. These signs may include separate sleeping and eating quarters or concealed accommodations.

Brief law enforcement staff and staff of other agencies about what to look for that may suggest isolation control when they are visiting premises.

Plan interviews to include questions that concern isolation control.

Religion, Culture and Belief Control

Victims of trafficking may have been prevented from taking part in religious services during their period of victimization. This can have a serious effect on the psychological well-being of those victims for whom religion is an important part of their lives.

In some cases religion has been used by traffickers to control victims. A commonly encountered example is that of African traditional religions and their derivatives that are found throughout parts of the Americas.

All of these present both challenges and opportunities for investigators. The attitude of the investigator is the key to meeting those challenges and maximizing opportunities. Specifically, you should have an open mind and approach this subject without prejudice.

Dealing with Control through Religion, Culture and Belief

Whatever your own faith, beliefs or opinions, they are unlikely to be reflected exactly by the faith, beliefs or opinions of the victims of trafficking you are dealing with. In some cases you may encounter beliefs that you find very difficult to understand. Whether you agree with the beliefs of a victim, you must work with them. A basic awareness of those beliefs, how those beliefs may have been exploited by criminals and what the effects are on the victim will help you prevent a possible block to your investigation. A deeper knowledge will give you some ideas of how to actively use religion and belief to support the victim and actively progress your investigation.

If a person of faith has been prevented from attending services and acts of worship, consider arranging for them to go to services or to speak to a religious leader.

This must be handled very carefully. If the religious leader does not understand the nature of trafficking they may display revulsion at what they hear or even condemn the victim for what they have been forced or coerced to do.

Anyone who is asked to speak to victims in this capacity should be clearly told they must keep all they are told confidential.

You may consider asking victims and religious leaders not to discuss with each other the exact details of the case under investigation.

Experience has shown that priests and elders of religions can help victims heal through counseling and explaining that whatever threats traffickers may have used to control the victims will not materialize.

CHAPTER 3

RECOGNIZING HUMAN TRAFFICKING AND IDENTIFYING VICTIMS

Human trafficking is often perceived by state and local law enforcement to be the primary or exclusive dominion of federal law enforcement authorizes. This may be due to a perception that the majority of victims are trafficked for the purposes of forced labor such as in agricultural work or sweatshop factories. However, the statistical majority of victims are trafficked for the purposes of sexual exploitation, the very nature of which causes the suspects and victims to be encountered during local law enforcement investigations.

The locations and settings where trafficking occurs do not always appear suspicious. For instance, trafficking could occur at places frequently visited by the public such as restaurants or hotels. Therefore, it is important to remember that the key indicators of this crime may not be in the setting itself, but in the conditions and circumstances of the labor involved. It is not possible to determine a situation of human trafficking based upon any single indicator.

State and local law enforcement officers may encounter the victims of human trafficking during "routine" calls for service. Law enforcement officers should consider the possibility that several different types of calls for service may involve some form of human trafficking or may be situation in which victims and/or traffickers could be found. The following are just a few examples of where officers may encounter human trafficking victims:

- Missing/run-away juvenile investigations
- Prostitution investigations
- Child abuse investigations
- Disturbances at hotels/motels
- Domestic disturbances
- Massage parlor inspections

Who Are the Victims of Human Trafficking?

Human trafficking is a horrific international problem with nearly a million victims trafficked across international borders annually. Victims can be trafficked into the U.S. from anywhere in the world. Victims come from, among other places, Africa, Asia, India, Latin America, Eastern Europe, Russia and Canada. More than half of those trafficked into the United States are children, although many women and men are victims as well. Many victims brought to the U.S. do not speak English and are unable to communicate with service providers, police, or others who might be able to help them.

However, this is not just an international problem. Within the U.S. both citizens and non-citizens all prey to traffickers. The U.S. State Department estimates that between 18,000 and 20,000 victims are trafficked into this country each year. Non-citizens and foreign victims are more susceptible than U.S. citizens to labor trafficking, and although labor trafficking can happen to U.S. citizens, more adult and child citizens are found in sex trafficking. Research indicates that most of the victims of sex trafficking into and within the United States are women and children.

Trafficking Networks

While there are some reports of kidnapping for the purpose of human trafficking, including reports of parents selling their children to traffickers, it is likely that most victims are recruited through fraud, deception, and other enticements which exploit legitimate financial and social needs. A human trafficking recruitment scheme does not necessarily begin with violence or coercion but rather as a confidence game. The victim typically believes desirable employment awaits them in a foreign country where the wages and standard of living are higher. At the point of recruitment the victim is convinced by the perpetrators that he/she is going to participate voluntarily in a smuggling scheme in which they will incur a debt in return for being brought into the destination country. In some cases the victim actually enters into a written or oral contract and "loaned" the money to facilitate their entry.

There are several key elements and often times multiple players involved in the trafficking of human beings. The logistical elements may include transportation and delivery/marketing, leading to the final exploitation of the victim.

Transportation

One of the major methods for human trafficking into the United States is through commercial aviation. Traffickers tend to use known transportation routes and frequently use the services of a travel agency in the source country which may or may not be linked to the larger criminal organization. In addition, traffickers use a number of ruses to assist the victim into the country such as applying for visas and then simply overstaying the visa. Victims may be transported across borders with or without legitimate immigration documentation. The use of stolen or forged documents and visas and the use of tourist visas are common. Military bases are popular points of entry into the county as service members can be compromised with offers of money or sex to bring their "brides" or "fiancés" back with them after an overseas deployment.

Delivery / Marketing

Even before the victim arrives in the United States, their services can be marketed through traditional outlets including advertising in personal columns. However, the most effective advertising is in digital media such as internet chat rooms, bulletins boards, matchmaking services, and other well known commercial sex providers such as myredbook.com and eros.com.

When a prior arrangement has been reached, the victim may be handed over to their intended employer upon arrival at the destination. Forced prostitution may or may not be confined to a particular ethnic community, however trafficking victims to a particular group further isolates the victim and increases their dependence on the criminals. Some victims are specifically marketed to a community where the victim has no common heritage, ethnicity, or language to dissuade them from seeking assistance.

Even if the victim is marketed to a particular ethnic group or community he/she may be moved frequently between cities. This technique accomplishes three things for the trafficker: it makes detection by local law enforcement difficult and serves as an impediment to multijurisdictional investigations; it provides a variety of victims to established customers; and it inhibits the victim from establishing ties to the community. This technique works equally well with illegally smuggled victims as well as domestic trafficking victims.

Exploitation

Non-citizen trafficking victims are in a precarious situation for three main reasons. First, as illegal immigrants, many victims are unaware of their rights as victims and are fearful of seeking assistance from law enforcement or other service organizations. Second, victims and potentially their families are frequently in debt to the traffickers who exploit them. Finally, revelation of the victim's participation in an illegal or socially stigmatizing trade such as prostitution may become known in the victim's home country significantly damaging his/her family's honor and reputation. Subsequently, those who take advantage of human trafficking victims maintain tremendous control and their "employment" becomes virtual slavery. Compounding the problem is that although their current conditions are bad, victims of trafficking may prefer their exploited employment status to horrific conditions they left in their home country.

Organized Trafficking Networks

Force, fraud and coercion are methods used by traffickers to press victims into lives of servitude and abuse. Human traffickers commonly use physical abuse such as rape, beatings, and confinement to restrain their victims. But how do the victims get there in the first place? Two the most common methods are through fraud and coercion. Fraud and coercion can occur through a variety of pretext offers designed to play on the victim's desire for a better life for themselves and their family. Direct recruitment of victims can come through schemes involving employment agencies or other offers of employment, modeling agencies, career fairs, educational opportunities, illegal foreign adoptions, Internet recruitment, friends and family, and other victims. Traffickers may also attempt to recruit their victims by befriending, romancing, or seducing them.

While domestic human trafficking is often limited to the pimp and the victim, international human trafficking can be much more complex and involve a greater number of people. For example, a 2004 study by the National Institute of Justice identified highly specialized roles and responsibilities associated with Chinese human trafficking organizations.

Recruiters are often relatives or close friends of the would-be immigrants who somehow know the smugglers. They may or may not have any further involvement in the smuggling operation.

Coordinators are central figures in smuggling operations because they have the connections to acquire necessary services for a fee. Their survival depends on their relationship with other partners who have access to those services.

Transporters help immigrants leave and enter countries. China-based transporters get immigrants to the border or the smuggling ship. U.S.-based transporters take smuggled immigrants from air- ports or seaports to safe houses.

Document vendors are well connected and able to produce documents to facilitate the transportation of immigrants. Some documents are authentic, obtained through official or unofficial channels, while others are fraudulent.

Corrupt public officials are the authorities in China and many transit countries that are paid to aid illegal Chinese immigrants. Some corrupt government officials act not only as facilitators but also as core members or partners of a smuggling organization. Subjects who belonged to large smuggling groups often indicated that local Chinese officials headed their groups.

Guides are responsible for moving illegal immigrants from one transit point to another or assisting immigrants who are entering the United States.

Crew members are employed by traffickers to charter or to work on smuggling ships.

Enforcers mostly are illegal immigrants themselves who are hired to work on the smuggling ships. They maintain order and distribute food and drinking water.

Debt collectors are based in the United States and are responsible for locking up illegal immigrants in safe houses until their smuggling fees are paid. Additional debt collectors are based in China.

Indicators of Trafficking Victims

These indicators outline some of the factors which may be present when a person is the victim of trafficking. These are general examples that may not apply in every case of trafficking.

Different types of trafficking; such as labor or sex related may produce different victim profiles. Even the same general types of trafficking may have significant differences in relation to location.

These indicators should be combined with available intelligence to create a specific profile for your jurisdiction. For those agencies in the initial stages of investigating human trafficking in their communities, some of these indicators may be helpful in identifying a new or emerging trafficking problem.

Age

The typical age range of suspected trafficking victims in a particular locality depends on the type of trafficking and the demand for those victims. With some exception, the older the person is, the less likely they are the victim of trafficking. This is particularly true in sexual exploitation cases. Traffickers will not normally victimize older people for sexual exploitation because of the minimal demand for their services. The same general rule is also applicable to labor exploitation because older victims are less productive. Minor children are particularly vulnerable to trafficking as they are more compliant and can be exploited across multiple markets in the illegal sex industry and labor markets.

Gender

Sex trafficking predominantly affects females and is present in virtually every country in the world. Male trafficking for the purposes of prostitution, particularly of teenage and younger boys, has been found to exist, but research and knowledge in this area is limited.

Trafficking in persons for labor exploitation affects both males and females. The proportions vary according to the form of the labor and prevailing gender roles at the location.

Location/Country of Origin

Many trafficking victims come from developing countries or countries in conflict where legitimate employment opportunities are limited. The supply chain of victims relies on a combination of factors including poverty, various types of discrimination, and the lack of opportunity.

However, not all victims come from "third world" countries. Developed countries also import and export trafficking victims for the purposes of sexual or labor exploitation. Typically these victims tend to come from vulnerable or disadvantaged populations within the countries.

Documentation

A person using another person's identification or travel documents at a border crossing or during routine law enforcement contacts is a general indicator of human trafficking. Additionally, the lack of identification of travel documents on a suspected victim, or fraudulent documents, are also strong indicators of potential trafficking.

Last location

The location where the victim was last, prior to coming to the attention of law enforcement may be significant. For example, discovery in a brothel or prostitution front or employment in sweatshop related industries such as restaurant kitchens or agricultural sites may be additional indicators of potential victimization.

Transport

How a person is, or has been, transported may be an additional trafficking indicator. Some characteristics of transportation of trafficking victims are similar to those found in migrant smuggling but there are a number of potential differences. For example, traffickers will commonly attempt to control all aspects of transportation from origin to destination because they only profit once the victim arrives at the destination location and the exploitation begins. However, migrant smugglers will typically have received all or part of their fees from their "customers" before they leave the country of origin.

Other transportation indicators of trafficking include evidence that the victim or victims is constantly escorted or under surveillance. The level of supervision will likely increase the closer the victim gets to their destination. This increasing control may be required in instances where it was initially easy to deceive the victim but they suspect, or realize, they are going to be exploited once they arrived at the destination. The traffickers will commonly use increased supervision as a control mechanism.

Anecdotal evidence from some international law enforcement agencies suggests traffickers frequently will use one transportation route for an extended period of time. This may be due to the often complex logistics involved in arranging international transportation through multiple countries.

Observations

Law enforcement officers may encounter the perpetrators or traffickers themselves who will offer alleged explanations of the situation. In these cases it is important for the first responding officer to note the following non-verbal clues about others at the scene of the crime who may be victims of human trafficking.

- What are their living conditions?
- What are their working conditions?
- Are there indications of restriction of movement (e.g., are they allowed to leave the premises)?
- Are there indications of frequent movement between locations/states?

- Is there a lack of private space, personal possessions, and/or financial records?
- Do they have access to a telephone?
- What are their methods of transportation?
- Are there any behavioral indicators of severe dependency (e.g., submissive behavior, fearful behavior in the presence of others)?
- Does it appear they have no or limited knowledge about how to function or navigate in a community?
- Who is in physical possession of their legal documents of identification?
- Is anyone in possession of false or fraudulent documentation?
- Who insists on providing information to law enforcement?
- Are they in the country legally?
- Are there any signs of physical abuse?
- Who speaks English? Is it just the "spokesman" or "manager"?
- Are they recent arrivals from source countries such as Asia, Latin America, Eastern Europe, Canada, Africa, or India?
- Do they appear to be under the age of 18?
- Does the "family" relationship make sense?

- Do they live in or near the workplace?
- A person who works excessive hours and is fearful of discussing working conditions or is unaware that certain unsafe conditions are unlawful
- A person who works excessive hours but receives little or no compensation

Evidence of Control

Traffickers use various techniques to keep victims enslaved. Some traffickers keep their victims under lock and key, however, the more frequent practice is to use less obvious techniques to instill fear or establish control including:

- A person whose movement and activities appear to be closely controlled or monitored by another
- A person who has little or no idea where they are geographically located and is always transported to and from the work site
- An able-bodied person who apparently never leaves home unless escorted by the homeowner
- A person who is fearful of discussing their

relationship to a person who appears to have physical control over them

- A foreign national adult or minor who is not in possession of identifying documents he or she claims to own and declares that someone else holds the identifying documents
- Debt bondage in which the victim is saddled with financial obligations that they are honor-bound to satisfy
- Isolation from the public by limiting contact with outsiders and making sure that any contact is monitored or superficial in nature
- Isolation from family members and members of their ethnic and religious community
- Confiscation of passports, visas and/or identification documents
- Use or threat of violence toward victims and/or families of victims
- The threat of shaming victims by exposing circumstances to family
- Telling victims they will be imprisoned or deported for immigration violations if they contact authorities
- Control of the victims" money, e.g., holding their money for "safe-keeping"

- Forcing the victim to sign a "contract" (often in their native language)

Attractive Locations

Locations that provide cover for the deployment of trafficked women include the following:

- Communities that tolerate red light districts, strip clubs, and late night bars and clubs where domestic prostitutes are plentiful, internationally trafficked women can blend in without drawing much attention
- Old warehouse and manufacturing districts, where sweatshops can flourish out of sight of local communities
- Well-off suburbs, where residents employ domestic servants who may be trafficked
- Isolated rural areas, where trafficked women maybe employed as seasonal farm laborers or be used to provide sexual services to male seasonal laborers
- Locations close to poorly patrolled border entry points or in immigrant communities that are

neglected by local government

- Areas with large immigrant or foreign-born populations that may frequent establishments setup in culturally familiar styles

Location Clues

Human traffickers involved with labor camps or sweatshops often implement security measures intended to keep victims confined as evidenced by the following:

- Presence of surveillance cameras on the interior or exterior of a business or residence
- Barbed wire surrounding the facility
- Bars on the windows
- Self-contained camps
- Bouncers, guards, and/or guard dogs
- Shopping allowed only at a "company store"

Physical Indicators

In addition to some of the subtle clues that indicate someone may be a victim of human trafficking, there may be physical signs as well, including:

- Visible injuries from beatings with or without weapons used
- Signs of being exposed to torture (e.g., cigarette burns, welts)
- Brands, scars, or tattoos indicating someone else's ownership
- Signs of malnutrition

Other Indicators

Further investigation may reveal other evidence of organized trafficking including:

- One subject who is financially responsible for a variety of different prostitutes cellular phones
- Common ownership or rental of locations used for in-call prostitution
- One attorney or law firm who represents multiple victims or suspects detained in different location

- Citizen complaints regarding excessive taxi or vehicle traffic and/or heavy foot traffic

Jurisdictional Awareness

- Awareness of trends and issues in the local community can help with identifying factors which may contribute to human trafficking.

- Are local police aware of the problem of human trafficking?

- Is the community aware of the problem of human trafficking?

- Is there an active sex trade in the jurisdiction? If so, what form does it take? Street prostitution? Escort services? Brothels, massage parlors, strip clubs, late night bars? Are foreign women encountered in brothel raids?

- How much of the local sex trade involves recent immigrants or ethnic communities?

- Is there a hidden or rumored sex trade? Are there known telephone numbers and addresses?

- Is there a narcotics trade linked to the sex trade or to a particular locality?

- Are there local businesses that benefit from the sex trade or forced labor such as agriculture, manufacturing, employment agencies, the garment industry, bars and strip clubs, nails salons, hotels, and restaurants?

- Are there community organizations that specialize in caring for immigrants which may serve as an early warning indicator?

- Are there known smuggling operations, routes or entry points in or close to your locality?

- Does your department formally recognize the immigrant community and its problems? Have you attempted to develop collaborative partnerships to deal with such problems?

- If there is a red light district? What are business and community attitudes toward it?

Overt Marketing

- Are there advertisements in printed publications or on the internet from known prostitution fronts which advertise young appearing sex workers or do they feature exotic foreign characteristics?

- Are there advertisements in local newspapers or magazines, especially those marketed towards immigrant communities or in a foreign language, which offer menial employment at unrealistically high wages?

- Are there local websites or chat rooms which specialize in sexual services such as craigslist.com, myredbook.com, backpage.com or eros.com?

- Do advertisements for mail order brides appear in local newspapers and magazines, local free or community papers? Do the ads promise foreign women?

- Do escort services advertise overtly on the internet or other media? Does your agency monitor them?

Venues

- Are there buildings with heavy on-premises security, such as barred windows, locked doors, and electronic surveillance both inside and outside the location?
- Do massage parlors and brothels constantly move to different locations? What kinds of buildings or housing do they occupy?
- Are there locations where bars or sexually oriented businesses cater to a particular immigrant or ethnic community?
- Are the relocations where legal businesses (massage parlors, nail salons) maybe fronts for sex trafficking?
- Are there farms that require low paid workers or seasonal labor? How do they find and recruit their workers?
- Are there sweat shops in your area? Is there a garment district?
- Are there industrial based businesses that employ low paid workers and how do they recruit them?
- Are there employment agencies in your area? Do they place persons of foreign birth? In to what

kinds of jobs? Do they place individuals who speak little English?

- Are there travel agencies that promote match making or sexual tourism?

- Are there dating or escort services in your area that offer women of foreign birth?

- Are there massage parlors in your area? If so, are they licensed or supervised by local health authorities?

- Does your jurisdiction contain a run-down warehouse or manufacturing district?

- Are there suburbs where domestic servants are routinely employed?

- Is tourism a major business in your jurisdiction? Are there hotels, motels, or restaurants that suddenly appear to be employing foreign women as maids, waitresses, or kitchen help?

- Do certain employers recruit workers from local homeless shelters? Are homeless persons transported to remote locations to work?

- Are there bus stations or other public transportation hubs where runaway teenage girls tend to congregate?

Incidents, Offenders, and Victims

- Have prostitutes been assaulted or murdered? If so, were they foreign-born?

- Are there cases of drug use or dealing involving foreign women? Does drug dealing occur in locations close to areas where the sex trade supplied?

- Are there local prostitutes who are unable to speak English?

- Are prostitutes typically drug users?

- Do hospitals report battered women who maybe illegal immigrants?

- Are there local or ethnic healthcare providers who are "off-line" from the normal healthcare system?

- What information is collected by officers and others concerning prostitutes? Is background information collected, such as age, country or place of birth, and where and how they were recruited?

- What pricing system is employed in brothels? How much are prostitutes paid?

- Who are the pimps and brothel managers? Where do they come from?

- What are the backgrounds of the purchasers of sex? How do they find their "partners?" How do they reach the venue? Walk from local hotels? Drive from suburbs?

- Are other crimes reported in the areas where prostitution or forced labor is located?

- Are undocumented migrants frequent robbery victims?

- Do incidents of domestic violence occur where the wife is an immigrant?

- Do local domestic violence shelters care for immigrant victims?

Specific Victim Indicators

Certain victim populations may have additional specific indicators of victimization. Children who are trafficking victims may:

- Have no access to their parents or guardians

- Look intimidated and behave in a way that does not correspond with behavior typical of children their age

- Have no friends of their own age outside of work

- Have no access to education

- Have no time for playing

- Live apart from other children and in substandard accommodations

- Eat apart from other members of the "family"

- Be given only leftovers to eat

- Be engaged in work that is not suitable for children

- Travel unaccompanied by adults

- Travel in groups with persons who are not relatives.

The following might also indicate that children have been trafficked:

- The presence of child-sized clothing typically worn for doing manual or sex work
- The presence of toys, beds and children's clothing in inappropriate places such as brothels and factories
- The claim made by an adult that he or she has "found" an unaccompanied child
- The finding of unaccompanied children carrying telephone numbers for calling taxis

People who have been trafficked for the purpose of domestic servitude may:

- Live with a family
- Not eat with the rest of the family
- Have no private space
- Sleep in a shared or inappropriate space
- Be reported missing by their employer even though they are still living in their employer's house
- Never or rarely leave the house for social reasons

- Never leave the house without their employer
- Be given only leftovers to eat
- Be subjected to insults, abuse, threats or violence

People who have been trafficked for the purpose of sexual exploitation may:

- Be of any age, although the age may vary according to the location and the market
- Move from one brothel to the next or work in various locations
- Be escorted whenever they go to and return from work and other outside activities
- Have tattoos or other marks indicating "ownership" by their exploiters
- Work long hours or have few if any days off
- Live or travel in a group, sometimes with other women who do not speak the same language
- Have very few items of clothing
- Have clothes that are mostly the kind typically worn for doing sex work

- Only know how to say sex-related words in the local language or in the language of the client group

- Have no cash of their own

- Be unable to show an identity document

- There is evidence that suspected victims have had unprotected and/or violent sex

- There is evidence that suspected victims cannot refuse unprotected and/or violent sex

- There is evidence that groups of women are under the control of others

- Advertisements are placed for brothels or similar places offering the services of women of a particular ethnicity or nationality

- It is reported that sex workers provide services to a clientele of a particular ethnicity or nationality

- It is reported in some literature that sex workers are not observed to smile

People who have been trafficked for labor exploitation may:

People who have been trafficked for the purpose of labor exploitation are typically made to work in sectors such as the following: agriculture, construction, entertainment, service industry and manufacturing.

- Live in groups in the same place where they work and leave those premises in frequently, if at all

- Live in degraded, unsuitable places, such as in agricultural or industrial buildings

- Not be dressed adequately for the work they do: for example, they may lack protective equipment or warm clothing

- Be given only leftovers to eat

- Have no access to their earnings

- Have no labor contract

- Work excessively long hours

- Depend on their employer for a number of services, including work, transportation and accommodations

- Have no choice of accommodations

- Never leave the work premises without their employer

- Be unable to move freely

- Be subject to security measures designed to keep them on the work premises

- Be disciplined through fines

- Be subjected to insults, abuse, threats or violence

- Lack of basic training and professional license

The following might also indicate that people have been trafficked for labor exploitation:

- Notices have been posted in languages other than the local language
- There are no health and safety notices
- The employer or manager is unable to show the documents required for employing workers from other countries
- The employer or manager is unable to show records of wages paid to workers
- The health and safety equipment is of poor quality or is missing
- Equipment is designed or has been modified so that it can be operated by children
- There is evidence that labor laws are being breached
- There is evidence that workers must pay for tools, food or accommodations or that those costs are being deducted from their wages

Data

- Crime analysis, research, and other data sources may also provide indicators of human trafficking including:

- Booking data from local jails and other correctional institutions

- Census data on population growth in immigrant communities

- Data on migration patterns and labor issues

- Data on teenage runaways and homeless youth

- Federal and state labor department data

- Geographic indicators (e.g., highways, borders)

- Historical cases

- Historical media reports

- Information provided by former victims of human trafficking

- Local law enforcement intelligence on criminal group dynamics

- Local law enforcement intelligence on - Vice Activities

- NGO data on community groups

- NGO data on providing services to victims of crime

- Site surveys of manufacturing, agricultural, industrial, and corporate settings

- Strategic interviews of community members in suspected activity areas

CHAPTER 4

INVESTIGATING HUMAN TRAFFICKING

Experience has shown that employing a victim-centered investigation and prosecution model secures victims' trust and thereby fosters truthful statements. This approach includes establishing a rapport with the victim and discussing her involvement in commercial sex matter-of-factly and non-judgmentally, rather than attempting to secure an "admission" to facts that are most likely already known. This approach can also include focusing initially on less sensitive; though still important information before pressing for details on particularly traumatic or humiliating incidents, which are better explored after establishing rapport. Finally, officers who have collected evidence from documents (brothel ledgers, for example) and surveillance (photographs of victims being transported, for example) can use it to challenge those who refuse to be forthcoming.

Be patient. Victims of sex trafficking are not like other crime victims, who often actively seek to involve law enforcement. Obtaining truthful statements will often involve multiple interviews over weeks or months, as the victim begins to recover from her trauma. Sex trafficking victims are often most forthcoming once they realize that law enforcement will not return them to their traffickers, and once they see that officers are genuinely interested in and attentive to their well-being. Many traffickers tell their victims that the police will not help them and will be interested only in arresting the victims for engaging in commercial sex acts or for being undocumented. One primary goal of the interviewing officer is to prove the trafficker wrong by demonstrating respect and understanding of the traumas the victim has experienced. Focusing on this goal, rather than on attempting to press the victim into relating the full scope of her victimization right away, will increase trust and reduce the pressure to withdraw, falsely deny or fabricate.

Do not stop investigating because victims lie, especially early on. As discussed previously, victims may be traumatized or fearful of law enforcement officers because the trafficker may have threatened to harm them or their families if they are truthful. This may lead victims to deceive law enforcement, especially early in the process. Law enforcement officers should anticipate this and develop a plan for establishing the victim's trust in order to secure truthful statements.

If victims are moved to another location consider housing and interviewing victims separately. Attempt to observe their interactions with each other. Some women initially thought to be victims may themselves be sex traffickers or enforcers. Sex traffickers often use several techniques to support their exploitative practices. For example, a pimp may empower a one-time victim by giving her enforcement and monitoring authority over other women coerced into commercial sex. These women, if housed or interviewed with other victims, will often seek to impede the investigation. Consequently, when multiple victims are in the presence of one another, it is critical to observe their body language to determine whether they are looking to a particular individual for cues or signals. In addition, such women who are "promoted" to roles as monitors or enforcers of other victims may be observed going from room to room, speaking with each, and attempting to overhear the conversations of victims with investigators.

Once you think you have encountered a crime scene involving human trafficking, there are other key factors you'll need to consider when identifying potential victims and distinguishing them from the real criminals-their traffickers. A person who is trafficked may look like anyone you encounter at a crime scene, but being sensitive, asking the right questions and looking for small clues will help you identify those people who have been fraudulently induced, forced or coerced into a life of sexual exploitation or forced labor.

Basic Initial Questions for Victims of Trafficking:

- How did you get here?

- Where do you live, eat and sleep?

- Do you owe someone money?

- Is someone keeping your legal/travel documents?

- Were you threatened if you tried to leave?

- Has your family been threatened?

- Were you ever physically abused?

- Were you ever forced to stay in one place?

- Who are you afraid of?

Investigative First Steps

Corroborating Victims' Statements

Sex trafficking victims provide the most complete and compelling evidence for a successful prosecution. Law enforcement officers should seek to develop additional evidence—no matter how small—to corroborate victims' statements. This might come from the testimony of other victims and witnesses or from physical evidence.

Once you have found one victim, look for additional and "historical" victims. Sex trafficking operations tend to involve multiple victims because traffickers seek to supply their clients with new women. Even in cases where the trafficker is exploiting only one woman at any particular time, a history of exploiting victims is likely. Victims from the past are called "historical" victims. Identifying additional and historical victims is often key to developing a successful sex trafficking case for prosecution. Like all human trafficking cases, sex trafficking cases involve lengthy and often complex relationships between the trafficker and the victim. Frequently, the only people who know the facts of the exploitation are the traffickers and their victims. Although many sex trafficking operations keep cryptic or coded ledgers, few offenders keep detailed documentary evidence of their exploitative conduct. A client may see parts of the operation for a brief moment, as might a driver or a hotel operator. But it is the victim who has suffered the coercion and repeated sex acts, and thus her testimony most completely describes the sex trafficking operation.

Even if one victim's testimony seems less convincing for example, as a result of biases against women who have engaged in commercial sex or who have provided initially conflicting statements—the cumulative testimony of several women, each describing the trafficker's use of coercion and fraud, can be persuasive to judges and juries.

Victims often know the identities of other victims or have heard stories about them. Where practical, law enforcement agents might delay arresting the trafficker or raiding the operation until they have conducted surveillance of known locations for additional victims and defendants.

Law enforcement may also identify additional and historical victims through media coverage of the arrest of the trafficker. For example, after the publicized arrest of a sex trafficker in one case, local law enforcement received several calls from women who said they had escaped his operation and now felt safe coming forward. Although law enforcement must be careful not to generate undue community (and possibly jury) prejudice against an arrestee or to further traumatize victims through excessive publicity, responsibly written and measured press releases that provide a contact number for possible victims can lead additional victims to come forward and help corroborate case. The trafficker may also respond to media coverage by contacting and threatening known and unknown victims to dissuade them from coming forward or contacting other suspects to destroy evidence or produce an alibi.

Use covert methods and exhaust them before conducting a raid or arresting the sex trafficker. Many law enforcement officers, upon finding a credible victim of sex trafficking, seek to immediately raid locations the victim identifies and arrest the trafficker. Where there is evidence of immediate and ongoing physical harm of victims or the exploitation of children, immediate raids and arrests may be the only acceptable path. However, officers should look to gather as much evidence as possible before raiding a sex trafficking enterprise and thereby terminating its operation. This evidence is critical for corroborating testimony and determining the scope of the enterprise, including finding other commercial sex locations and victims.

Obtain and execute search warrants, and anticipate needing additional warrants predicated on facts you discover during the execution of the initial warrants (i.e., roll-over warrants). Photograph or film the exterior and interior of locations during execution of the warrants. The most significant corroborating physical evidence in sex trafficking cases typically is found in locations where victims have lived or engaged in commercial sex acts. Evidence may be documents and other items kept by the trafficker, such as debt and income ledgers, tally sheets, lists of telephone numbers and bank records. Equally important may be items kept by the victims, including diaries, provocative clothing, condoms, lubricants and sex paraphernalia. Also look for digital evidence in cell phones, iPods®, iPads® and laptops.

During these searches, officers typically find evidence of additional commercial sex locations and agents of the sex trafficker. In many cases officers have found addresses and telephone numbers of brothels and nightclubs where victims were taken to engage in commercial sex acts. Agents should be prepared to obtain roll-over warrants to search these locations, based on the evidence obtained in the initial search.

Photographs and film of the locations are also valuable evidence. For example, in one case in which traffickers were sentenced to 50 years in prison, officers filmed their approach to a basement brothel, their entry through a small door, and the squalid and crowded conditions inside. This kind of evidence proves particularly compelling to jurors and corroborates that the victims were not there willingly. Officers should also photograph locks and other restraints, and any posted rules or notices.

Take a broad view of leads. Victims often have some contact with people other than the sex traffickers and clients. For example, victims might be taken to a store to buy provocative clothing or to a club to meet prospective clients. Inquire about such activities when interviewing victims, and then interview witnesses who might have observed them. In one case, a store attendant testified that she observed the victims being monitored by the trafficker when they went into a changing room. In another case, a club doorman stated that the trafficker arrived at the club with the victims and that he controlled and monitored their movements and activities. Although these witnesses did not observe brutality or commercial sex, their evidence helped corroborate the victims' statements that they were being compelled and controlled by the trafficker.

Officers should also follow the money. Sex trafficking can generate substantial cash. Determine from victims and other witnesses whether bank accounts, wire transfers, deposit boxes or credit cards were used by the traffickers and seek to obtain the relevant records. Investigators should seize these funds so they can be used to fund restitution orders to compensate victims for their trauma.

Confidential Informants

Law enforcement has identified numerous sex trafficking cases based on information provided by confidential informants, such as taxi drivers, johns, bar patrons and others who have contact with commercial sex operations. Many traffickers operate in and target specific communities: construction workers from a particular region in Mexico, Korean businessmen or regular patrons of a particular nightclub. Because offers of commercial sex are not made to outsiders, such as someone with a different Mexican dialect; traditional "sting" or undercover operations often do not work in these environments. Instead, officers must identify and recruit people who operate at the fringes of these sex trafficking ventures. In one case, a taxi driver reported that he was receiving calls to pick up very young women from a particular address and deliver them to hotel rooms. Law enforcement worked with this informant to identify a network of houses where victims were held by pimps and other taxi drivers who were prostituting juvenile girls. The success of this approach hinges, of course, on an agency's ability to identify potential confidential informants.

It is important for investigators to keep good records about information received from confidential informants and if that information can be corroborated by other evidence. During the court process the trafficker may seek to have the identity of the confidential informant disclosed. The court will have to balance what information the informant provided, if that information could have been discovered by other means, if the information can be corroborated and any safety issues that may arise from disclosure.

Case Management

Identify all the players

Conduct pertinent background information checks:

- Criminal histories
- Prior calls for service
- Business records and licenses
- Financial Crimes Enforcement Network (FINCIN) information

Consider preparing a timeline/link analysis chart showing how long the victim lived where and with whom. Federal law enforcement agencies and Regional Intelligence Sharing Services can assist you with this.

Interview other witnesses.

1. Identify and contact other victims, if possible.

2. Re-interview the victim to clarify additional details, for example:

- What were the rules?

- What did the suspect promise? (family, wages)

- Was the victim not allowed to speak unless spoken to?

- Did the suspect provide fake names?

- Did the suspect require the victim to wear certain clothing?

3. Have the victim identify all of the locations of occurrence.

4. Contact former employees and other people close to the suspect(s).

5. Bring in specialized investigators, if appropriate.

Attempt to corroborate the victim's statements through:

a. Search warrants on bank accounts and other records to demonstrate how the victim was paid

b. Talk to family members, friends, and neighbors

c. Obtain border crossing records

d. Car registration records

e. Hotel / Motel registers

f. Phone records – Incoming / Outgoing Calls, Text Messages, Contacts, Photos

Complete background on the suspect. Interview, interrogate, and give Miranda/Beheler admonitions as appropriate.

Present the case to the prosecutor

a. If applicable, assist in coordinating the pre-file interview with the victim(s)

b. Provide information and feedback to assist the prosecutor in the victim credibility Evaluation

c. Complete supplemental investigative requests

The following key questions are guidelines to assist law enforcement during the interview process to help determine whether someone is a victim of human trafficking. Remember to use plain, simple language when interviewing victims. Try to use open-ended questions that do not suggest the answer. Consider follow-up questions asking, "Why?" particularly if you are only getting yes / no responses. If answers are inconsistent or illogical ask for further explanation. These questions and complete follow-up will help to secure information that can later be used as testimonial evidence.

Fraud/Financial Coercion Questions

- How did you get your job?
- How did you get into this country?
- Who brought you into this country?
- Did you come to this country for a specific job that you were promised?
- Who promised you this job?
- Were you forced to do different work?
- Who forced you into doing different work than what was promised?
- Was there some sort of work contract signed?
- Who organized your travel?
- How was payment for your travel handled?
- Are you getting paid to do your job?
- Do you actually receive payment or is your money being held for you?
- Do you owe your employer money?
- Are there records or receipts of what is owed to your employer/recruiter?
- Are there records/receipts of what was earned/paid to you?
- How were financial transactions handled?

- Are you in possession of your own legal (I.D.) documents? If not, why?
- Were you provided false documents or identification?
- Are you being made to do things that you do not want to do?

Physical Abuse Questions

- Were you ever threatened with harm if you tried to leave?

- Did you ever witness any threats against other people if they tried to leave?

- Has your family been threatened?

- Do you know about any other person's family ever being threatened?

- Were you ever physically abused, or did you ever witness abuse against another person?

- What type of physical abuse did you witness?

- Were there any objects or weapons used in the physical abuse?

- Where are these objects or weapons located?

- Was knowledge of this abuse ever communicated to a person outside of this situation (e.g., police reports, domestic violence reports, hospital records, social service records)?

- Was anyone else ever abused or threatened with harm in your presence?

- Does the trafficker have a reputation for violence? Are you aware of any specific acts of violence committed by the trafficker?

- How were medical problems handled, and who attended to them?

Freedom of Movement Questions

- Is your freedom of movement restricted? Can you come and go as you please?
- Were you asked to pay unreasonable fees to be transported to locations?
- Do you live and work in the same place?
- What were the conditions under which you were left unattended?
- Were there instances of physical restriction through locks, chains, etc.?
- Where are the locks used and who has the keys to them?
- How was movement in public places handled (e.g., car, van, bus, subway)?
- Who supervised your movement in public places?
- How was the purchase of private goods and services handled (e.g., medicines, prescriptions)?

- What forms of media or telecommunication did you have access to (e.g., television, radio, newspapers, magazines, telephone, the Internet)?

Psychological Coercion Questions

- Who are you afraid of?
- Why are you afraid of them?
- Do you love this person? Do you think he loves you?
- What would you like to see happen to the people who hurt you (e.g., jail, deportation)?
- How do you feel about the police? Why?

Environmental Indicators:

- Do you live and work in the same place?
- Where do you live/eat/sleep?
- Where do the alleged perpetrators live/eat/sleep?
- Are the living conditions between the two excessively disparate?

Law enforcement officers questioning the victim should consider the following:

Is there evidence of possible "Stockholm" or "Patty Hearst" Syndrome where the victim, because of his or her dependency, actually begins to identify with the trafficker?

Initial Victim Assessment

If someone insists on being the spokesperson for the victim, be very leery and separate that person from the others. It may be necessary to remove the victim(s) from the scene.

Allow the victim to describe the experience in his or her own words without interrupting. Use open-ended questions to clarify the details. If you need a translator to speak with a victim, be sure that translator is a law enforcement officer.

- I am here to help you.
- Tell me about your current situation.
- Is someone holding your documents?

- Did someone threaten to report you to the authorities?
- Is this the job you were promised or expected?
- Can you come and go as you please?
- Has anyone hurt or threatened to hurt you or your family?
- Who is your employer?
- Does your employer provide housing, food, clothes, or uniforms?
- Did you enter into an employment contract? What does it say?
- Do you owe money to your employer?
- Did your employer/boss tell you what to say to police?
- Were you forced to have sex as part of the job?
- Can you freely leave your employment situation and work somewhere else?
- Does your employer hold your wages?
- Are there guards at work or video cameras to monitor and make sure no one leaves?
- What would happen if you left the job?
- Have you been physically harmed? Have you been deprived of food, water, sleep, medical care, or other life necessities?

- Were you kidnapped or sold?
- Are you allowed to buy clothes and food on your own?
- Can you freely contact (phone, write) friends and family?
- Are you isolated from the community?
- Are minors allowed to attend school?
- How did you get to the U.S.?Did someone help you?
- Do you owe money for your trip?
- What did you think you were going to be doing?
- Can you come and go as you please?
- Are there usually people around, watching you?
- Do you have any papers? Who has them?
- What kind of work do you do?
- Are you paid? Regularly? How much?
- Is your boss holding your money?
- Do you owe money to your boss or anyone else?
- Can you leave if you want to?
- Has your boss or anyone else threatened to report you to the authorities?
- Do you feel scared?

- Has your boss or anyone else threatened to hurt you or your family?
- Has your boss or anyone else hurt you?
- Did you get medical care/ dental care/

Recording Statements

Procedures regarding recording all interviews with the victim, witnesses, and suspect depend upon individual departmental policies. Recording statements can be an excellent investigative tool. If possible, video record all interviews with victims, witnesses or suspects.

Advantages of recording statements include:

- Provides more detail than handwritten notes
- Enables investigators to be more attentive during the interview, assists investigators in synopsizing details
- Protects the interviewer should a complaint or misunderstanding arise
- Conveys the victim's immediate response to prosecutors and jurors

- Provides training material for use in improving the quality of interviews
- Disadvantages of recording statements include:
- May be intimidating to the victim and cause reluctance to disclose
- May highlight inconsistencies when taking multiple statements from victim

Types of Physical Evidence

Evidence that can be used against the trafficker includes the following:

Advertisements - There may be print advertisements in local or sex trade publications. Also consider advertisements on internet sites such as Craigslist and Red Book.

Airline and Bus Tickets - Trafficking victims are frequently moved to various locations to keep them isolated from other and dependent on the trafficker.

Apartment and Rental Property Leases – Often times, suspects will rent out apartments and single-family residences and utilized them as brothels and safe houses. Court orders can provide valuable information as to who is renting a location, which often times is someone hired by the organization as to not directly connect the suspects to the operation. Discovering the identity of renters can be valuable in including them as conspirators in the investigation and turning them into witnesses on the behalf of the prosecution. These parties can also provide information to your investigation that corroborates victim and suspect statements. If you are obtaining this information prior to a sting or search/arrest warrant, be sure that you do background checks on the property owners. Should you suspect that the owner of a property might be involved in the criminal enterprise, it's often best to hold off in obtaining the information as a follow-up investigation.

Bank Records and Receipts - Human trafficking and the exploitative acts the victims are forced to engage in can generate substantial amounts of cash. Traffickers will frequently deposit the money into bank accounts or wire transfer the money to other co-conspirators. Have federal partners check all of the suspects in the Department of the Treasury's Financial Crimes Enforcement Network (FINCEN).

Business Ledgers and Cards - Traffickers are often responsible to others in the organization and may keep business ledgers to account for funds derived from their activities. Victims may also keep their own ledgers, be sure to compare with the suspect's ledgers also. Suspects may also have business cards for "front" businesses.

Business Licenses - Many times traffickers will use a quasi-legitimate business as a front for prostitution or labor trafficking. These traffickers will obtain business licenses and fictitious business name statements as "proof" their businesses are legitimate. A search of county or city databases may uncover other previously unknown businesses.

Car Registration – It is important to establish current and prior cars owned by the trafficker. In some cases traffickers use "associates" cars. Registration records may not only corroborate a victim's statement but may also establish accessories to the trafficking.

Cell Phones - Cell phones are a critical component of human trafficking investigations. In one investigation the madam used ten different cell phones - one for each house of prostitution. A thorough analysis of cell phone records can assist investigators and prosecutors with identifying other victims and unidentified co-conspirators. Cell phone analysis is also helpful in tracking a victim or suspect's whereabouts.

Client Lists - Traffickers commonly maintain lists of preferred or vetted clients for easy reference. These lists can be compelling evidence and may lead to additional witnesses who are willing to cooperate in lieu of prosecution. Commonly these will be stored electronically and within cell phone contact lists.

Computers - Computers are frequently used to post advertisements in the personal sections of some websites. Forensic examination of suspects" computers can lead to valuable evidence and provide new leads.

Contracts - Traffickers sometimes have "contracts" between them and their victims. These documents may be in the victim's native language.

Criminal History – Prior crimes or convictions by the trafficker that are known by the victim may help establish or corroborate the timeline of exploitation. The traffickers' criminal past may also help confirm if there is a history of weapons use or access to weapons.

GPS - Outcall prostitute sometimes make use of GPS devices to get to unfamiliar locations. Forensic tools exist to recover the memory of these devices.

Hotel/Motel Receipts/Keys - Victims of sex related human trafficking are commonly moved from location to location. The suspect may have receipts showing they rented the rooms and/or keys showing their dominion and control over the room.

Identification and Immigration Documents (real and forged) - driver's licenses, Social Security cards, passports, birth certificates, visas, green cards, work permits, evidence of forgery, stolen ID's. It is not uncommon for the suspect to hold onto the victim's identification documents in order to maintain control over them. They may also possess multiple false identifications for themselves and their victims.

Narcotics - Some traffickers use narcotics and other legitimate medications to sedate their victims or to maintain control over addicted victims.

Personal - As a method of control victims are usually not allowed to keep many personal possessions. They may however have retained copies of the advertisements they initially responded to and copies of work agreements or contracts. They may also keep letters of even a journal.

Phone Calls - Initial 911 calls for service, recordings of jail calls made by the suspects, and/or pretext phone calls between the victims and the suspects.

Photographic / Electronic / Print Media - CD-ROM/DVDs, Websites, Internet accounts, email, Web bulletin boards, chat rooms, personal ads, matchmaking services, flash drives, including those on key chains. Identifying websites where advertisements are made of victims – always follow-up with search warrants on website advertisements as they can often lead to information that links a suspect to a criminal enterprise through financial transactions and email accounts.

Physical Attributes – Traffickers may use tattoos to brand their victims with a moniker or other symbol to identify them as their property. Tattoos on the trafficker may also be used to corroborate the victim's statement, particularly if the trafficker claims no knowledge of the victim or if the tattoo is in an intimate place that cannot generally be seen by the public. Traffickers also may change their physical appearance in an attempt to hide from law enforcement or disrupt identification by victims.

Physical Evidence - Common paraphernalia associated with human sex trafficking include condoms, lubricants, sex devices, and provocative clothing.

Pictures - In order to post electronic and print advertisements traffickers frequently take pictures of their victims. These pictures may be stored in digital cameras, cell phones, and/or computers. When dealing with juvenile victims, provocative photographs in the suspects possession can lead to child pornography charges.

Surveillance Videos - Some prostitution locations are equipped with surveillance systems to alert the proprietor of law enforcement's presence. These systems can be used against the trafficker by showing the comings and goings of customers and the suspects themselves. Traffickers also use surveillance systems as a form of supervision of their victims.

Utility Bills - Utility bills can tie a trafficker in to a particular location or lead to other locations that the trafficker might have utility services at (i.e. other brothels, safe houses and residences).

CHAPTER 5

CRIME SCENES, PHYSICAL EVDENCE, AND EXAMINATIONS IN HUMAN TRAFICKING INVESTIGATIONS

Introduction

Physical evidence is sometimes overlooked in human trafficking investigations. However, physical evidence is particularly important when it reinforces the victim's statements. The two primary questions to address when considering physical evidence and crime scene examinations are:

- What are the goals of the examination?
- How are you going to achieve it, given the available resources and circumstances of the case?

What are the goals of the investigation?

There are a number of potential goals you may wish to achieve from a forensic examination in a human trafficking case. These include:

- Identifying suspect
- Identifying a victim
- Establishing the age of a victim;
- Corroborating a victim's account;
- Identifying the links between suspects, victims, locations, vehicles, documents, etc.
- Identifying the authenticity of identity and travel documents

How are you going to achieve it?

An important initial consideration is the resources available to your agency during the investigation. Some of the technologies and resources needed to complete the investigation may not be available or may be cost prohibitive. This may require the assistance of other law enforcement agencies, including those of the federal government. It's always best to have an investigative plan that covers the involvement of multitude of agencies and specialties.

Crime Scene Examination and Physical Evidence

A crime scene is anywhere that contains records of past activities. A crime scene can be a location, vehicle, or person, including victims and suspects.

A crime scene investigation is an examination of the scene using an approved technical and scientific approach. The examination of a crime scene is predicated on the fundamental principle of forensic science that every contact leaves a trace.

Specific features of crime scene examinations in human trafficking

Crime scenes in human trafficking investigations present a number of challenges to law enforcement personnel. There may be a different response from the victims of human trafficking versus traditional crime scene investigations. Language barriers may exist between investigators and crime scene personnel and the victims. Initial victims' interviews may provide only vague suspect descriptions or names and vague or inaccurate details of past locations. Investigators and crime scene personnel may have no, or limited exposure, to human trafficking cases and may be unaware of the various types of physical evidence available or where to locate it. There may also be types of evidence which are not traditionally collected during "routine" crime scene investigations including communications equipment such as cellular phones and lap top computers requiring forensic examination and financial documents for forensic auditing.

You should always consider what scenes might be linked and where those scenes might be located. The location of the sex trafficking, the living quarters of the victim, the suspect's residence or business, and vehicles used to transport the victims will all require simultaneous management. They will also likely produce opportunities to collect additional evidence. However, care should be taken to prevent the potential for cross contamination of evidence from one crime scene to another.

One of the main differences in investigating human trafficking crime scenes versus other cases is the potential of seizing and collecting a large number of items for forensic examination. The chain of custody in a human trafficking case may be long and complex because there may be a need to transfer evidence between multiple jurisdictions and investigative agencies.

Many general crime scene investigations consist of a single short lived event. In human trafficking cases the crime is likely to be a complex series of events involving exploitation over a long period of time in a number of different locations and potentially involving multiple suspects. An unfortunate consequence is that many scenes which may have contained valuable forensic or trace evidence have been compromised to the point where even if located it would likely be inadmissible.

Types of Physical Evidence in Human Trafficking Investigations

General considerations

The determination to obtain forensic evidence should be made early in the investigation. Failure to collect the evidence in a timely manner can result in challenges to its admissibility during prosecution.

It may not always be clear who is a suspect or victim during the initial stages of the investigation. In fact this may not become apparent for some time. Because of this when you are conducting interviews of potential suspects or potential victims it is important to use legal precautions, such as informing the interviewee of their Miranda rights, so the statement is not compromised.

There may be instances where forensic evidence alone will substantiate a victim of human trafficking have been assaulted, but this is likely to be the exception not the rule. In many cases forensic evidence will act as corroborative evidence for the victim statements or other evidence.

The value of forensic victim examination may be limited because the victims and the traffickers often have long term close contact with each other. In some instances the victim may be involved in an intimate relationship with the suspect.

Sexual Assault Examinations

- Where a victim is to be examined, it should only be done with his or her consent.
- If possible the victim should be allowed to choose the gender of the forensic medical examiner.
- Where a child victim is involved consent should always be obtained from the child's parent, guardian or other independent adult official who has temporary parental rights and responsibilities in respect of the child. Consent should be obtained before an examination takes place.
- The victim must be told what the examination will consist of and why an examination is required before he/she gives her consent. Consent is not genuine if the victim does not understand

what he/she has agreed to.

- In the case of a child the explanation should be given to the parent or guardian but every effort should be made to help the child understand as much as possible about the examination and why it is being conducted.

- Every effort should be made to provide proper clothing for the victim if his/her own clothing is to be removed: crime scene paper overalls or jail clothing is not suitable forms of clothing.

- Do not transport victims in the same vehicles as suspects or detain them in the same place as suspects; doing so may transfer forensic evidence from suspect to victim or lead to allegations that this has happened.

- No one who has been to a location where an offence is alleged to have happened should come near the victim before clothing has been removed or the examination has taken place because they may be transferring material from the location to the victim. The same advice applies to going near to suspects before they are examined.

- Many victims may have physical or psychological impairments (or both). Examination for evidence of crimes should not take place before the victim has been assessed by a suitable medically qualified person to establish if she is well enough to be examined.

- If possible clothing should not be removed before forensic examination. Consider photographing the victim before clothing is removed.

- If clothing has to be removed it should be removed in a place and way that allows the victim to keep his/her dignity.

- Members of the opposite sex should not be present when clothing is removed. Clothing should be removed and packed in a way that preserves evidence.

- Examinations should only be conducted by properly qualified people, often doctors or nurses. Where a country has laws or procedures that govern examinations these should be complied with.

- Every effort should be made to examine the victim promptly.

- Where it is not possible to do a full forensic examination you should consider what you are able to do with facilities you have available such as taking photographs and clothing.

- You may be able to obtain samples from some types of offense by using non-intimate techniques that can be used by investigators. An example is a mouth swab for DNA, etc. in cases where oral sex is part of the offense. Care should be taken to ensure this is allowed under local legislation.

- Many victims are likely to want to wash, either because of the sex offense committed against them or because their traffickers have not allowed them to wash for some time. Washing may remove evidence and victims should be discouraged from washing until they have been examined. This must be explained as compassionately and sensitively as possible.

- Allow victims to wash if they insist after it has been explained this may remove evidence. Eating, drinking, smoking or washing teeth may also remove evidence of some types of sexual offense (oral sex for example). Victims may not have eaten properly or drank for some time and may want to do so. Any request for the victim not to eat, etc. should be balanced with an assessment of what evidence you think would be realistically obtained.

- If doing any of things above appears likely to cause the victim to stop cooperating you should decide whether the evidence you are likely to get justifies the risk of withdrawal of cooperation.

Objectives of forensic examination in sexual exploitation cases include:

- Any injuries consistent with the allegation, for example injuries to genitalia.
- Information that shows the extent of the injuries. This might include the severity of recent injuries or old injuries that have healed to some extent.
- The presence of traces of other people on the victim.
- Obtaining samples to link the victim to other locations, people, etc.
- Remember to ask her to indicate if she has other clothes and if so where they are. Record or photograph the clothes where they are when you find them so you know where they are and try to seize this clothing for possible forensic examination.
- Showing that a particular individual had sex with or

sexually assaulted a victim.

- Showing that a particular individual physically assaulted a victim.

- Corroborating a victim's account of what happened to him/her.

- Identifying any injuries, illness or disease that may be related to their exploitation.

- Establishing how long a person has been victimized.

- Establishing the age of injuries to a victim.

- Identifying the victim.

- Establishing the age of the victim.

- Connecting a victim to a particular location, vehicle, etc.

- Identifying any drugs or alcohol administered to or taken by the victim.

Examining victims

- Informed consent of the victim for purposes of examination may be difficult to obtain in a timely manner because of victim traumatization, difficulty in translation, and fear or mistrust of the police.

- If it is not possible to conduct a full examination consider undertaking a less intrusive examination. Although this may not prove contact with an individual it may give corroboration of the victim's account, for example showing visible injuries consistent with what she is saying.

- If a full examination has a secondary objective of corroboration of the victim's account, the presence of semen from many men would be valuable to asexual exploitation investigation even if you cannot identify the men.

- In sexual exploitation cases under clothing can be particularly useful to obtain traces of semen that has drained from victim.

- In many trafficking in persons cases a victim may be disclosing an incident that took place sometime a go and no samples remain.

- The effects of victimization may mean accounts from suspected victim's sexual exploitation are particularly vague and incomplete.

- Victims of trafficking in persons for sexual exploitation may have had sexual contact with many people with the possibility that samples from many people are present on those victims.

- Semen may be found in the vagina, anus, mouth or virtually any other part of the victim.

- Hairs, both pubic and head hair will be transferred between the victim and the suspect. Victims may not have had access to clean clothes for some time. Numerous forensic traces may be present on the clothing.

- Examination is likely to be invasive and maybe a pointless further victimization of the woman.

- For the reasons outlined above, there may be cases where a physical examination of a victim of sexual exploitation for trafficking in persons is unlikely to reveal any evidence of practical value. Investigators must (in consultation with forensic and medical experts) decide if the potential results of an examination justify asking a victim to consent to physical examination.

Actions

- Approach a human trafficking crime scene using the standardized crime scene investigation methods.
- Take appropriate health and safety precaution while trying to avoid stigmatizing the victim.
- Record where a person was on first encounter and what they were doing at the time.
- Record the general scene where a possible victim was found. This should be done using cameras and videos where available, drawings, plans and written descriptions.
- It is strongly recommended that before starting the examination of a victim you should establish what the victim's account is and what else is known about things like the location she was found in. Finding out what is being alleged should always be balanced with the need for the recovery of evidence which may be rapidly disappearing or deteriorating.
- Although trace transfer is more likely the longer a person is in the company with another there may be traces of certain material in locations on a body

that are difficult to explain no matter how long they have been in contact.

- Obtaining a full account helps to identify those areas for examination where a trace would corroborate the account.

- You may consider a medical examination to establish age of victims. You should be aware this can be very difficult and may not be accurate.

- Make a note, draw or photograph the victim showing any visible injuries. Even where a victim consents to having non-visible injuries examined and recorded it is good practice to photograph or keep a record of how they were dressed before the examination. Whatever the extent of the examination the person consents to any record of injuries, etc., will add to the investigation.

- When taking photographs, be aware that showing a victim's face may cause problems in some cases. The defense may have access to the photograph or video leading to revelation in courts or to the suspect. Taking pictures of faces may reduce the changes of cooperation.

- Examination of clothing may reveal useful samples. Even where you are able to examine it is good practice to seize clothing.

- Clothing may be available for examination that the victim is not wearing at the time.

- Clothing may also have visible damage that corroborates the victim's account.

- Bedding (see "Locations" section below for more detail) and other furniture may also yield samples of value.

- In all cases investigators should try to identify where the victim's clothing is, where he or she slept, other areas of premises they had access to, worked or lived in, vehicles travelled in, etc., to increase forensic opportunities.

- Obtain control samples from the victim. Ideally this should include fingerprints, DNA and hair samples. These are required link to victims to locations etc.

- Collect any documents (identity, travel documents and all other type of documents).

Forensic Age Assessment

The age of a victim is very significant in many jurisdictions because it affects the charge and eventual sentence. It also has a significant impact on the victim care that the person is entitled to. In some locations there have been issues with corruption of examiners to give an older or younger age as suits the "traffickers" purposes.

In some locations there are no birth certificates and there is the possibility that parents may be involved in the trafficking. Some form of forensic examination may be the only option you have to establish age.

Similarly, identification of the victim using identity documents and identification by relatives may be problematic because the documents never existed or have been destroyed. Relatives can be unwilling to help because they are colluding with the traffickers or they are afraid.

Teeth are useful in estimating individual's age as the development and formation of teeth is relatively independent of the external or nutritional status of an individual. This is an important aspect of trafficking in persons investigations, especially when trying to identify children. Age is an important factor as it impacts upon the legal status of the individual and subsequently what care protection would be required.

It is essential that only experienced and independent dentists are allowed to use this means to assess the age of a person.

An experienced dentist can accurately estimate a child's age by looking at:

- The number and quality of fillings;
- Presence of plaque and calculus, cavities, gingivitis and periodontitis;
- Amount of dental wear;
- Type of teeth present;
- Tooth color;
- Recessions;
- The number and type of teeth present in the mouth.

However, when trying to determine someone's age other methods should also be taken into account such as:

- A psychosocial age assessment (e.g. inspection of physical appearance, interviewing the victim);

- Physical and radiological examinations of (*a*) the hand/wrist of the non-dominant hand and (*b*) the medial ends of both collar bones as well as (*c*) the radiological examination of the dentition.

Examination of suspects

General Considerations

- It may not be clear who is a suspect or victim on first encounter.

- Suspects may resist attempts to detain or search them or seize their property.

- Suspects may be in possession of weapons or other items that they could either deliberately use on those searching them or which could cause injury during a search.

- You may have some knowledge of what is alleged to have happened before you encounter the suspect either through a victim or witness account or the result of other enquiries.

- Examining suspects - specific considerations in sexual exploitation cases.

- Allegations of sexual assault are likely to leave samples of the victim on the suspect on intimate parts of a suspect's body (as well as the rest of the body).

- Alleged sexual assaults may have taken place some

time ago.

- Although traces of suspects on victim's bodies may be discharged, degraded quickly or washed from their traces of the victim may remain on the suspect's body for some time, particularly where the suspect has poor hygiene.

- While it can be argued a trace has been found because victims and suspects live or work in close proximity, some traces are in locations on bodies and are difficult to explain away by "innocent contact."

Actions

- General crime scene approach applies in examinations of suspects.

- Plan your forensic strategy around what you are aware of already. Continually review what you know and amend the forensic strategy accordingly. It is recommended you work with forensic examiners and analysts when making these decisions.

- In all searches of people think health and safety.

- Record where suspects are found, for example

where they were in a building, where they were sleeping, where they were sitting in a vehicle, etc.

- Record who was with the suspect at the time he or she was encountered.
- Where possible record this with video or photographs.
- Photograph how they are dressed clothing.
- Search clothing - look for documents, phones and weapons.
- Do so in a way you are not going to contaminate it or lose material.
- Record what is found and who it is found on, preferably with photo/video if you can.
- Record any injuries visible when the suspect is clothed.
- Consider seizing the clothing of suspects. Do this in accordance with your legislation and in a way that protects the dignity and privacy of the person. It is best to seize clothing at a police station or similar place. If you do have to seize clothing "in the field," ensure it is done at a location and in a way that avoids cross-contamination and protects the person's dignity.

- If suspect(s) and possible victims are found keep them separate as far as possible (this is a good practice not only for forensic purposes but to prevent intimidation).

- It may be inevitable that there is some cross - contamination when suspects and possible victims are found together. Do what you can to ensure initial searches are conducted by separate people. Keep a record of who searched who and by open with forensic examiners, prosecutors and courts about what happened.

- Where appropriate, consider a full physical examination of the suspect conducted by an appropriately qualified person. This should be done in accordance with your legislation.

- Obtain fingerprints from suspects. This will allow you to link them to particular equipment, documents or locations.

- Consider obtaining DNA where appropriate. This may have an application in detecting who sent letters, etc.

Specific Actions in Sexual Exploitations Cases

- Consider conducting an intimate examination of the suspect by an appropriate person in accordance with your legislation.

- Work with the person conducting the examination to identify objectives and main areas of interest in the examination.

- Examinations of locations

Considerations

Many locations in trafficking in persons cases will carry health and safety risks to investigating personnel. In many human trafficking locations there is likely to be significant contamination of scenes with multiple traces.

In many encounters it may be difficult to identify who are exploiters and who are victims. This may not become apparent until sometime later. On most premises there will be a very large number of fingerprints. Recovering all fingerprints may be difficult, time consuming and involve specialist techniques.

In a trafficking in person's case you may need to secure a location for a long time to plan and complete a forensic examination.

Specific Considerations in Sexual Exploitation Cases

- Body fluids and traces are likely to be present at brothels and similar locations. These may present a significant risk to health and safety.

- Brothels are likely to have many DNA samples present in traces of semen, blood, other body fluids and material.

- Documents of interest include any accounts or other records that show prices for sexual services and details of things like "rent" paid. Experience has shown that in many situations of commercial sexual exploitation quite detailed records are kept. Where the location is a brothel, make a record of reception areas, public rooms, cubicles, etc.

- Bedding is likely to reveal many contact traces. Consider seizing bedding, etc. Seizing it allows the option of examination. If full examination does not prove practical, the condition of the bedding may be valuable in corroborating an account, etc.

- Record any sex toys, sexual implements, lubricants or similar material and seize them. These may be evidence in of themselves, but also give opportunities for finger mark and DNA evidence recovery.

Actions

- General crime scene approach applies to examinations of locations.
- Use existing information and intelligence to plan a forensic strategy when entering premises, both in the case of tactical entries (raids) and visits on follow-up enquiries.
- Record who is present and what they are doing when you enter a location. Ideally this should be photographed or videoed, and diagrams should be drawn.
- Ask people to identify where they work or sleep. Record their responses. Consider identifying who slept at a particular location, by photograph where possible, or other techniques such as fingerprinting the area of the bed or seizing bedding where appropriate.
- Consider interviewing those on the premises to establish who has access to where and for what

purpose.

- Documents of interest should be sought on premises, recorded and where appropriate, seized for possible further examination. Examples include any notices showing regulations, services offered, identity and travel documents, records of employment ledgers and similar recording transactions.
- Any suspected drugs or other substances of interest found should be recorded and retained for possible analysis.
- Active review should take place to take account of any new information that emerges.
- Computers, laptops, cell phones should be seized.

Examinations of Vehicles

Considerations

- Vehicles may offer a useful opportunity to link victims to suspects and vice versa.

- Upholstery in cars and other vehicles may contain hairs and fibers from clothing from both victims and suspects.

- Property in vehicles such as receipts for gasoline, parking tickets, etc., may also offer good opportunities for examination.

- Litter in cars such as cigarette butts, and candy/food wrappers, may offer opportunities for examination.

- Most vehicles carry registration or license plates which allow tracing.

- Documents such as driver licenses and insurance certificates are required to drive and operate vehicles.

- Some traffickers will use vehicles without documents, but others will drive legally as they do not wish to attract law enforcement attention.

- Even where no index number is available it is possible to trace vehicles through combinations of color, manufacturer and individual marks. In some locations this can be done by automated searches.
- Vehicles can be removed by law enforcement and kept until they are able to examine it.
- Some vehicles may contain equipment that allows you to track its movements such as GPS navigations systems.
- If the vehicle itself does not have equipment that allows tracking, the people in it may have used or be using mobile phones that can allow tracking.

Specific Considerations in Sexual Exploitation Cases

- If there is an allegation of sex or sexual assault taking place in a vehicle, semen and other material of interest may be left.
- Where there is an allegation of sex or sexual assault taking place in a car, forensic personnel should be informed. If forensic examiners are not aware of the nature of the allegation examination will not take place

- Where taxis and other forms of public transport are used, consider checks of driver's duties, calls for cabs, etc.

In trafficking cases in some locations there a number of very short journeys from where the victim is living to where they are being exploited, often by taxi.

Examinations of documents found at the scene, on victims, on suspects and in vehicles

Considerations

Trafficking in persons is a commercial process and as in any type of business, records must be kept. These records are frequently very valuable for investigators. Forensic investigations present a number of opportunities to determine the authenticity of a document or the author of a handwritten document or note.

Examples of significant documents that may be found in trafficking in persons investigations include:

- Bank statements and details of informal transactions
- Accounts of money taken in brothels or other illegitimate businesses
- Utility bills such as gas, electricity or phone bills
- Records of rent paid, details of landlords, etc.
- Tickets, boarding passes and other travel documents

- Records of bills paid for advertising
- Credit card details of customers
- Documents giving work instructions or "menus" of "services" available
- Photographs of employees
- Identity documents both genuine and counterfeited/forged
- Cash
- Documents in factories and other work places that record details of people working at a location
- Documents that show the volume of trade in a particular location, such as material brought in and finished goods dispatched

Specific Considerations in Sexual Exploitation Cases:

Records may still be kept even by brothel keepers and similar even where prostitution is illegal. Examples include price lists, records of cash receipts, how many "clients" have visited a particular woman.

Document Evidence

The illegal reproduction or manufacture of identification and travel documents are important evidence in human trafficking investigations. Documents can be counterfeited forged, or obtained through identity theft. Evidence of counterfeiting and forgery may exist in the documents themselves and the data processing equipment used to produce them. Other documents relating to the recruitment and transportation of the victim may exist at the crime scene or the residence or business office of the suspect. There may be additional evidence found in business and financial records maintained by the suspect.

Actions

- Documentary evidence should always be handled with gloves;
- Depending on the type of fraud or type of document involved the first examination will be done at the first line of inspection, in the field, the two first bullet points:
- Visual examination of features without specific equipment: e.g., watermarks, relief structure, mechanical erasure;
- Examination of features with technical facilities (e.g., visible light, UV, IR): e.g., fibers, chemical eradication;
- Examinations in the forensic science laboratory with sophisticated equipment that cannot be used in the field
- Actions specific to sexual exploitation cases when examining documents

Always seize anything that appears to be a record, no matter how informal that record may look

Examinations of computers and communication equipment found at the scene, on victims and suspects and in vehicles:

Considerations

- Computers and communication equipment are essential to both legitimate and criminal organizations and present a number of forensic investigation opportunities including:
- Records of calls made, numbers held, photographs and videos, etc. - on phones, both mobile and fixed-line.
- Similar records from fax machines, pagers and phones which record messages.
- E-mails, bank details, advertising material, accounts, etc., held on computers, including desktop, laptops and small personal devices.
- Diaries and similar. These may include personal organizers, Personal Digital Assist- ants (PDAs), Blackberries, notebooks, iPhones, etc.

CHAPTER 6

THE VICTIM'S PSYCHOLOGICAL REACTIONS AND IMMEDIATE NEEDS

Most victims of trafficking will have suffered one or more traumatic events and will have adopted psychological tactics to cope with the effects of these events. To begin to understand these reactions, it is important to first understand a bit about "trauma."

What is trauma?

According to experts on trauma:

> *"The essence of trauma is that it overwhelms the victim's psychological and biological coping mechanisms. This occurs when internal and external*

resources are inadequate to cope with the external threat."[2]

Traumatic experiences suffered by victims of trafficking in persons are often complex, multiple and can occur over a long period of time. For many individuals who are trafficked, abuse or other trauma-inducing events may have started long before the trafficking process.

Studies of trauma in cases of trafficking in persons have been conducted, but there are few of them. Studies so far tend to focus on trafficking for sexual exploitation, but are yet to cover victims from every origin location. However, they offer some guidance and conclusions, especially when they are considered in conjunction with what is generally known about trauma and anecdotal evidence from around the world. It is essential you are aware of these conclusions and you are able to identify how they might affect your work as a criminal justice practitioner.

No two victims of trafficking are the same and the impact trafficking has upon each individual varies. You cannot make assumptions about how individuals might or should react. You must treat each person as an individual and on his or her own merit.

Individuals will react to you in different ways. Do not expect a victim of trafficking to see you as their rescuer or savior: Some might, but many may see you as an unwelcomed intruder, which may further compound what is already a very complex situation.

If a victim reacts in a hostile or aggressive way, it may have nothing to do with you as a person, your role or the organization you work for. Victims may have adopted these tactics and emotions to cope with or to survive their ordeal. It is likely that they would react to anyone in the same way.

Not every victim will react to the investigation with hostility, but many will. Do not see this as your fault or that of the victim and do not respond to any hostility in a negative way. If you do, it is very unlikely you will be able to build up the necessary rapport with the victim.

Challenging and direct questioning too early is very likely to alienate the victim and may re-traumatize the victim. Challenging a victim's veracity, treating the victim as a suspect or showing doubt or signs of disbelief are likely to remind him or her of the defensive position they held during the trafficking ordeal. This is likely to destroy any chance of cooperation. Avoid this approach at all costs. A considered, methodical and non-judgmental approach has the best chance of revealing the truth whatever it may be. In most cases, you will have an opportunity to express your concerns or doubts at a later date.

You are unlikely to have encountered people who have suffered the range of chronic abuses found in trafficking victims. Nonetheless, there might be some similarities with cases you have dealt with previously. Victims of chronic domestic violence have often suffered similar levels of assault, abuse and control to those experienced by victims of trafficking for sexual exploitation.

Levels of psychological trauma experienced by some victims (either before or during the trafficking process) may be so high that they are never going to be able to serve as witnesses in court or even give an account that can be used as the basis of intelligence. You should always be prepared to terminate an interview if necessary and seek immediate assistance for the individual. On the other hand, it is also possible that some individuals who initially present strong emotional reactions, may, with time and professional support or counseling, become perfectly capable witnesses.

Common traumatizing experiences of victims of trafficking

There are two factors that are said to be most predictive of a strong reaction to ongoing trauma:

- Unpredictability of events
- Uncontrollability of events

These two characteristics are perhaps defining features of a trafficking situation, particularly the latter.

The following list describes the forms of control very commonly used by those in possession of a trafficked person.

Restriction of Movement

Control may by definition, is the trafficking process that involves removing control from victims. This applies to all forms of trafficking. Control has been found to cover all aspects of life, even the most intimate: when a victim eats, goes to the toilet, works, sleep, where they go, who they are with. In some cases, victims may have been controlled from the outset, for example if they have been abducted. In other cases, control may have been relatively weak in the early stages but increased as the victim went through the trafficking process, becoming strongest as they near and reach the destination location/exploitation phase be subtle, involving direct or implied threats or making the victim feel responsible for their own behavior. Sexual exploitation victims may be given a small amount of money for what they do; others may be involved in petty crime such as stealing from shops, street begging or working in illegal industries, for example drug trafficking. This can lead to feelings of guilt and loathing, which makes it even more difficult to tell anyone what has happened.

Levels of control may differ according to the type and perpetrator of trafficking in persons. In trafficking for sexual exploitation, studies have shown that in some locations only 3 percent of victims reported that they were "always free." Some comments by this 3 percent revealed a different story; however, for example "I was always (free) I could go out when I wanted to, but only with someone."

Controls of this scale and intensity mean that victims can become fearful or incapable of making decisions, even the smallest decisions

Violence

Victims may have been subject to violence before and during the trafficking process. Violence before trafficking has been seen in a substantial number of victims of trafficking for sexual exploitation, with around 60 percent reporting experiencing some form of violence before trafficking in one study. Pre-trafficking violence in other forms of trafficking has not been researched.

Once engaged in the trafficking process, victims may be subjected to a range of violent acts from threats to serious assaults. Again, the intensity of violence varies. In sexual exploitation cases, up to 70 percent of women have reported physical violence and 90 percent sexual violence while being trafficked. Children recruited/abducted to fight as soldiers have been controlled by beatings and rape. The picture in domestic servitude cases is not clear, but anecdotal evidence suggests that assault is commonly used by "employers" to control victims.

Threats of various kinds are used frequently by traffickers to control victims and can target the victim, their family or friends. The threats may be of direct violence to a particular person or a threat to expose the victim to the authorities, for instance, where they are in a location illegally or have been involved in criminal activity. Threats may be implied, for example, arranging that the victim witness the abuse of another individual in the same circumstances or simply making the victim aware that the trafficker is part of a very violent gang.

The power of these threats should not be underestimated. Even where the traffickers are not in a position to carry out the threats, the victim may believe they are. Victims may have been brought across many miles and territories by a gang who appears powerful, sophisticated and organized with links in many locations; these links may include law enforcement and other officials. Traffickers may have demonstrated they are capable of violence.

Eighty-nine percent of women interviewed in one study of trafficking for sexual exploitation said they had been threatened while being trafficked. In a significant number of cases, the families of victims or people they knew had been involved in their trafficking.

Abuse

Victims may have experienced abuse falling short of direct physical violence before and during trafficking. Abuse should be understood widely, for example, to include verbal or psycho- logical abuse, deprivation or other controlling or harmful behaviors that negatively affect an individual.

In some locations, victims of trafficking have been found to come from dysfunctional backgrounds before they were trafficked. Examples include victims whose parents were addicted to alcohol or drugs, experienced or witnessed domestic violence, were orphaned as children, were homeless, or whose health and safety have been affected by dire conditions, war, civil unrest, poor diet or lack of access to education.

During the trafficking process, victims may have been forced to work very long hours with limited breaks. They may not have had access to nutritional food, protective equipment, adequate amounts of fluids or clean clothing and the means to wash themselves or medical care.

Multiple Traumas

As you read throughout the sections of this guide, you begin to understand how trafficking in persons investigations differ from other types of investigation. One significant difference between the trauma in these cases and many others is that victims have suffered multiple, often ongoing traumatic events during numerous periods of their lives, perhaps by multiple perpetrators. While this should not be seen as minimizing the trauma found in other cases, experiencing multiple or chronic traumatic or abusive events has been found to have more negative effects than a single trauma.

A victim's anxiety can be complex to unravel, as many victims still face real dangers related to their trafficking experience even after removal from the site of exploitation. It is necessary here to recall that in one study on trafficking in women, 89 percent of the women were threatened while in the trafficking situation, and 36 percent reported that traffickers threatened their families. In addition, many were trafficked by family members or someone from their place of origin. Studies have shown that trafficked women continue to receive threats by phone and in-person, both against themselves and their families, and that protection by authorities has been extremely limited. For this reason, when a person exhibits fear and anxiety, it is necessary to consider that this may very well be the victim's sensible response to actual danger.

Consequences for criminal justice practitioners

This section will discuss issues around obtaining an account from a person suffering from the range of symptoms experienced by victims of trafficking who have been sexually abused or sexually exploited.

Behavior of the Victim

The behavior of the victim could include:

- Hostility towards the investigator or prosecutor.
- The victim may have learned that anything jeopardizing the dominance of the traffickers could lead to immediate violence. She or he may thus avoid any cooperation with law enforcement or judicial authorities;
- Failure to cooperate with the investigation or prosecution;
- Memory loss, lapses, discrepancies, resulting in changes in the account at different times or an inability to recall details

- Ability to recall central details of a traumatic incident, but not peripheral details such as descriptions of clothing, rooms or vehicles
- Blocking out events that were most life threatening (e.g., dissociation)
- Outbursts that appear to be irrational;
- Disorientation after leaving the situation of ongoing trauma and control;
- Continuing anxiety despite apparently being "safe";
- Needing more breaks, rest and sleep than might be expected;

Often times a single victim will exhibit more than one of these reactions. A victim who is seemingly strong and cooperative one day is hostile and unavailable the next. Attempting to understand the victim's trauma and anticipating these changes is crucial.

Reconstruction and Remembering

For many victims, there is a period of re-construction as they process what has happened to them. Victims re-interpret events and try to come to terms with their experience, to possibly find an explanation for what has happened, or to evaluate the event.

What you should do (and not do)

- Take the victim to a secure environment away from traffickers or those associated with traffickers.
- Avoid early interviews wherever possible. An early interview of the victim will in many cases overstrain the victim's capacity to remember and to cope with the over whelming memories and may jeopardize the consistency of the statement you obtain.
- Victims should be stabilized before they are interviewed in detail about what happened to them. This stabilization may involve working with healthcare professionals (medical assessment and treatment for both medical and psychological symptoms), social support workers and those who

193

provide accommodations and counseling services.

- When you interview the victim, organize a comfortable and safe interview setting, including dressing plain clothing. Where an initial account is required this should be freely recall and (wherever possible) without challenge. Keep in mind though that the victim may say something that needs corroboration and/or clarifying to prevent harm coming to them or others.

- During the interview, use simple measures such as choice in food to help return a sense of control.

- Start planning for accommodations and support as soon as you can. Contact and coordinate with local organizations or state agencies to establish working relationships and plans for accommodations and support before you become involved in a trafficking investigation. In this way, you will have options available through organizations who have tentatively agreed to assist. If you are involved in a proactive investigation, do these from the outset; if it is a reactive investigation make early plans as soon as you realize you may need to accommodate the victim.

- If you can, take measures to prevent harm on those

under threat such as family members or other loved ones of the victim.

Avoid secondary victimization

Secondary victimization refers to the victimization that occurs, not as a direct result of the criminal act, but through the response of institutions and individuals who are insensitive to the needs and vulnerable status of the victim. The whole process of criminal investigation and trial may cause secondary victimization, because of difficulties in balancing the rights of the victim against the rights of the accused or the offender, or even because the needs and perspective of the victim is entirely ignored.

Meeting The Victim's Immediate Needs

Victims of human trafficking are vulnerable human beings who have been subjected to severe physical and emotional coercion. These trafficking victims are usually in desperate need of assistance. Victims of human trafficking need to be assured that once they come in contact with law enforcement officers, they should feel protected and safe.

There are benefits and services available to trafficking victims. And the Trafficking Victims Protection Act (TVPA) authorizes special benefits and services to adult victims who are willing to cooperate in the prosecution of their traffickers and to minor victims regardless of whether they are willing to cooperate. These benefits and services include legal, healthcare, counseling, housing, food, medical, cash and employment assistance.

Needs of victims of human trafficking may include:

- Case management.
- Civil legal restitution.
- Clothing.
- Criminal justice assistance.
- Crisis intervention.
- Dental (emergency and long-term).
- Disability assistance.
- English as a Second Language (ESL) classes.
- Family contact/reunification.
- Food.
- Healthcare.
- Housing.
- Identification documents.
- Illiteracy or limited literacy assistance.
- Job preparation and placement.
- Legal assistance.
- Medical (emergency and long-term).
- Mental health (emergency and long-term).
- Religious and spiritual assistance.

- Repatriation assistance.
- Safety.
- Shelter.
- Sexual assault trauma services.
- Substance abuse services.
- Translation and interpretation.
- Transportation.
- Victim advocacy.

Resources

There are a variety of resources available to law enforcement officers investigating human trafficking cases.

Federal

Federal Bureau of Investigation (FBI) Victim-Witness Coordinator

Each FBI field office has a victim-witness coordinator who specializes in victim assistance at the investigative stage. They can be reached through the headquarters victim-witness staff at 202-324-6360 during regular business hours.

United States Attorney Law Enforcement Community Coordinator

In each state, this individual can address the particular needs of your department and find the appropriate agents, offices, and resources within the federal government. The liaison is accessible through the local U.S. Attorney's office.

United States Attorney Victim-Witness Coordinator

The victim-witness coordinator in your area is responsible for organizing victim and witness services with federal and local law enforcement officials. They can obtain victim services in multiple jurisdictions and can be helpful for providing services in rural and remote areas. The coordinator is accessible through the local U.S. Attorney's office

United States Immigrations and Customs Enforcement (ICE) Victim-Witness Coordinator

There are over 300 ICE Victim - Witness Coordinators throughout the U.S. who assist with victim needs and services. They are trained on the crime of human trafficking. For a referral to your local victim witness coordinator, call the ICE toll free number 866-872-4973 during regular business hours.

National Trafficking in Persons Worker Exploitation Task Force Complaint Line

This line can provide immediate translation services in over 150 languages. Law enforcement officers can also call this number for assistance in deter-mining if a case may be trafficking. By providing information gathered through victim interviews, the call taker will complete an assessment or intake and connect you with federal law enforcement partners. The hotline is open during normal business hours. If all lines are busy, leave a message and your call will be returned within 24 hours.

Call 888-428-7581 or visit www.usdoj. gov/crt/crim/tpwetf.htm.

National Human Trafficking Resource Center

The National Human Trafficking Resource Center (NHTRC) is a national, toll-free hotline (1-888-3737-888), available to answer calls from anywhere in the country, 24 hours a day, 7 days a week, every day of the year. The NHTRC is a program of Polaris Project, a non-profit, non-governmental organization working exclusively on the issue of human trafficking. The NHTRC takes tips about potential situations of human trafficking and facilitates reporting to specialized human trafficking task forces, federal authorities, local law enforcement, and service providers throughout the country.

Through its extensive contacts database, the NHTRC helps connect survivors of human trafficking with services, including case management, emergency shelter, legal services and counseling. The NHTRC also assists organizations who serve victims by providing referrals to services and resources, and helps to connect community members with volunteer opportunities.

Call Specialists can answer your questions about human trafficking and can respond to requests for information about a diverse array of topics. Our online library contains relevant materials useful to community members, students, and professionals interested in learning more about the issue of human trafficking.

The NHTRC provides training and technical assistance through the hotline that seeks to build individual and practitioner expertise and strengthen local anti-trafficking infrastructure to improve the nationwide response to human trafficking.

Freedom Network

The Mission of the Freedom Network Training Institute (FNTI) is to uphold and enforce the human rights principle that all human beings have the right to live free from forced labor, slavery and servitude. The FNTI holds the core belief that collaboration among the trafficked person, law enforcement, social service providers and community organizations is central to the problem of modern day slavery for both prevention and elimination.

The FNTI is the training arm of the larger Freedom Network USA, a group of over 25 member organizations engaged in a critical and immediate struggle to free those who are held captive here in the United States and work towards long-term strategic systemic changes to better protect workers. These organizations provide advocacy, direct social and legal services and inform policy throughout the country.

Activities

Since 2003 the FNTI has been working to build awareness and educate communities, organizations and law enforcement about the crime of Human Trafficking and Modern Day Slavery. The FNTI has trained thousands across the country. Not only does the training utilize facilitators who are experts in the subject and work directly with survivors of the crime, but it links practical tools and information to real case examples from the field. The intensive training includes a thorough rights based, client centered approach to what modern day slavery is and what the root causes are, how to identify workers held in slavery, how to investigate a slavery operation (law enforcement), and how non-governmental organizations, law enforcement, and the survivors themselves can collaborate on bringing justice and freedom to workers" lives. The FNTI brings together disparate groups that normally wouldn't be in a room together-law enforcement, service providers, community based organizations, policymakers, and community stakeholders and educates them on: 1.) the

Human Rights approach to workers rights and human trafficking, 2.) the comprehensive definitions of modern day slavery/trafficking, 3.) practical steps to follow, 4.) best practices in service delivery, 5.) the necessity for collaboration, and 6.) how this knowledge informs best practices in legislative advocacy.

The strength of the FNTI program is that the facilitators of the trainings come from around the country, are social service and legal service providers and have worked with multi-disciplinary teams to uncover slavery operations, and provide assistance throughout the life of a case. This firsthand experience coupled with a firm grasp of the issues of immigration, migration, labor, trauma and the law results in a dynamic, informative and useful one or two day program that meets the needs of all first responders and the community at large.

FNTI Approach

FNTI works steadily to ensure trafficked and enslaved persons can pursue legal and social justice through the collaboration among the trafficked person, law enforcement, and social service providers. Many people who have escaped slavery want to see justice done and help other workers still held captive by participating in the criminal prosecutions of abusive employers. The only institution with a mandate to do criminal prosecutions is the government. Accordingly, not only community and grassroots organizations need FNTI training, but also police officers, government prosecutors, FBI and Immigration agents must understand the importance of using human-rights based approach in their treatment of survivors.

Training law enforcement is so critical that the FNTI developed a specialized program. *"Human Trafficking and Slavery: Law Enforcement Tools for an Effective Response"* is used to train law enforcement to treat enslaved and trafficked persons as victims of a crime, not as criminals. The core FNTI curriculum, *"Human Trafficking and Modern-Day Slavery: Practical Tools For An Effective Response"* can be used for multi-disciplinary participants as it contains the four basic modules of *Dimensions of Human Trafficking, Identifying Trafficked Persons, Social Services and the Legal Framework.*

The Social Service and Legal Framework Modules also have expanded versions for those particular participant groups desiring more detail.

Following training by the FNTI, an organization/s may request ongoing technical assistance from us. This can include help with capacity building, step by step progression through a new case, links to necessary partners, additional training opportunities, sharing of materials, and general guidance. The FNTI has provided this all important on-going technical assistance to many organizations and various law enforcement entities. It is not unusual for a Federal agency to reach out to the FNTI and ask for our assistance in the many trainings conducted for Immigration Customs and Enforcement agents, Department of Justice investigators and prosecutors, the Office for Victims of Crime and Department of Health and Human Services social and legal service providers. We are able through these trainings to promote our comprehensive approach to trafficking and our human rights framework.

Immigration Relief

Some of the trafficking victims in the United States are aliens (noncitizens) who are illegally present (i.e., unauthorized/illegal aliens). Some of these aliens entered legally, but overstayed their length of legal admittance. Other aliens were smuggled into or illegally entered the United States, and then became trafficking victims. In addition, some aliens have had their immigration documents confiscated by the traffickers as a form of control. The lack of immigration status may prevent victims from seeking help, and may interfere with the ability of the victim to provide testimony during a criminal trial. As such, under law, there are certain protections from removal (deportation) available to noncitizen victims of trafficking.

T-Non-immigrant Status

The Victims of Trafficking and Violence Protection Act of 2000 (TVPA) created a new nonimmigrant category, known as T-status or T-visa, for aliens who are victims of severe forms of TIP. Aliens who received T-status are eligible to remain in the United States for four years and may apply for lawful permanent residence status (LPR) after being continually present in the United States for three years.

To qualify for the "T" category, in addition to being a victim of a severe form of TIP, the alien must be physically present in the United States, American Samoa, the Commonwealth of the Northern Mariana Islands, or a U.S. port of entry. Because of such trafficking including physical presence on account of the alien having been allowed entry into the United States for participation in investigative or judicial processes associated with an act or a perpetrator of trafficking; have complied with any reasonable request for assistance to law enforcement in the investigation or prosecution of acts of trafficking unless unable to do so due to physical or psychological trauma, or be under the age of 18; and be likely to suffer extreme hardship involving unusual and severe harm upon removal.

To receive T status, the alien must also be admissible to the United States or obtain a waiver of inadmissibility. A waiver of inadmissibility is available for health related grounds, public charge grounds, or criminal grounds if the activities rendering the alien inadmissible were caused by or were incident to the alien's victimization. Waivers are not automatically granted, and there is no appeal if the inadmissibility waiver is denied. This waiver is especially important for those involved in sexual trafficking since prostitution is one of the grounds of inadmissibility specified in the Immigration and Nationality Act (INA). Additionally, aliens who are present without being admitted or paroled into the United States are inadmissible and would need to obtain a waiver to be eligible for T status. For example, an alien who paid a smuggler to enter the country illegally and then was held in servitude would need to get an inadmissibility waiver to be eligible for T status.

T-status is limited to 5,000 principal aliens each fiscal year. Additionally, the spouse, children, or parents of an alien under age 21, in order to avoid extreme hardship, may be given derivative T-status which is not counted against the numerical limit. Individuals who are eligible for T-status may be granted work authorization. T-status is valid for four years, and may be extended if a federal, state, or local law enforcement official, prosecutor, judge, or other authority investigating or prosecuting activity relating to human trafficking certifies that the presence of the alien in the United States is necessary to assist in the investigation or prosecution of TIP.

Under law, aliens who have bona fide T applications are eligible to receive certain public benefits to the same extent as refugees. Aliens who receive derivative T-status (i.e., the family members of trafficking victims) are also eligible for benefits. In addition, regulations require that federal officials provide trafficking victims with specific information regarding their rights and services such as immigration benefits; federal and state benefits and services (e.g., certification by the Department of Health and Human Services [HHS] and assistance through HHS's Office of Refugee Resettlement [ORR]); medical services; pro-bono and low cost legal services; victim service organizations; victims compensation (trafficked aliens are often eligible for compensation from state and federal crime victims programs); the right to restitution; and the rights of privacy and confidentiality.

U-Nonimmigrant Status

Some victims of trafficking are eligible for U-nonimmigrant status. The Violence Against Women Act of

2000, Division B of TVPA, created the U-nonimmigrant status, often called the U-visa, for victims of physical or mental abuse. To qualify for U status, the alien must file a petition and establish that he/she suffered substantial physical or mental abuse as a result of having been a victim of certain criminal activities; as certified by a law enforcement or immigration official, he/she (or if the alien is a child under age 16, the child's parent, guardian or friend) possesses information about the criminal activity involved; he/she has been, is being or is likely to be helpful in the investigation and prosecution of the criminal activity by federal, state or local law enforcement authorities; and the criminal activity violated the laws of the United States or occurred in the United States.

The U category is limited to 10,000 principal aliens per fiscal year. After three years, those in U status may apply for LPR status. Unlike aliens with T status, those with U status are not eligible for assistance through the Office of Refugee Resettlement or for federal public benefits. Those who receive U status may be eligible for programs to assist crime victims though the Department of Justice's Office for Victims of Crime.

Applicants for T-status may submit a Law Enforcement Agency (LEA) to prove that they are complying with the investigation. The regulations require that the LEA enforcement come from a federal law enforcement agency since severe forms of trafficking in person are federal crimes under TVPA; however, the TVPRA of 2003 amended the law to allow state and local law enforcement to certify that the trafficking victim is aiding law enforcement.

Community Resources

Here are some of the local resources NGOs can use for victims:

Food: Food pantries; soup kitchens; faith-based food programs; supermarkets/ restaurants/bakeries providing day-old, slightly damaged, or leftover food items to charitable organizations

Shelter: Domestic violence/women's shelters; runaway and homeless youth shelters; transitional housing programs; shelters for undocumented immigrants (usually for men); and faith-based housing programs, such as the Catholic Worker Movement that provides housing opportunities in many U.S. communities (http://www.catholicworker.org/communities/commlistall. cfm); some faith-based organizations donate rent money or identify church members who can offer temporary housing; temporary shelter in seminaries, convents, or school dorms; State foster care for eligible children; state or local housing and community development agencies can provide lists of affordable housing projects and identify non-profit organizations that manage affordable housing

Clothing and Goods: Local chapters of national organizations providing clothing and goods (Goodwill, Salvation Army, St. Vincent de Paul, AMVETS Thrift Stores); many nonprofits operating thrift stores offer free clothing giveaways; professional clothing donation services, such as local Dress for Success® affiliates (http://www.dressforsuccess.org/dfs_affiliates.aspx) or The Women's Alliance (http://www.thewomensalliance.org/):similar locally operated programs can be found through Internet search engines; some churches, schools, and hospitals operate clothing drives/clothing banks; refugee resettlement agencies provide donated goods; yard sales are excellent sources for inexpensive used clothing and household goods; many department stores give away damaged and out- of-season clothing to charitable organizations; community dry cleaners may operate clothing donation drop-off sites; hotels may donate old furniture when renovating or they may be willing to provide shampoo and other toiletries; sexual assault crisis center clothing collections; churches, businesses, and civic organizations may be willing to donate gift cards for grocery stores or discount department stores

Medical: Community health centers; migrant health clinics; city clinics; homeless clinics; free clinics at universities or in communities; health fairs at community hospitals (for preventive services); county mental health clinics; health programs operated out of NGOs; substance abuse services; maternal and child health programs; parenting classes

Legal: Legal aid clinics/agencies/foundations; law school clinics; pro bono services offered by law firms; employment law centers; community-based legal providers, such as those serving particular ethnic communities;

immigration rights clinics; nonprofit organizations providing legal assistance to immigrants; faith-based immigration relief organizations, such as the Catholic Legal Immigrant Network, Inc. (CLINIC), which provides support services to diocesan and other affiliated immigration programs, with field offices in 48 States (for a listing of CLINIC members, go to http://cliniclegal.org/ and click on the icon "Public Directory Clinic Members")

Job Training Programs: Local affiliates of Goodwill Industries offer job training programs (http://www.goodwill.org/goodwill-for-you/jobs-and-careers/);

Career One Stop (http://www.careeronestop.org/) lists local contacts for apprenticeships and employment assistance; vocational training and job placement assistance are offered by community colleges and immigrant or refugee assistance organizations

Education Services: GED assistance and general educational assistance programs at local adult education centers; immigrant community organizations; city/neighborhood community centers; ESL (English as a second language) classes held at churches, schools, libraries, community colleges; translation/interpreting services (written/live language assistance; native tongue literacy)

Transportation: Clients enrolled in education programs can sometimes qualify for lower fares for public transportation, such as the subway, bus, or train, with a student ID; voluntary driver programs (often operated out of churches); car and bike donation programs

Crime Victim Compensation: Clients can usually apply at the city or county levels; funds can be used to pay for many of the above services, including relocation costs for safety reasons (see U.S. Department of Justice programs discussed later in this booklet)

Other Assistance: Battered immigrant women's programs; sexual assault coalitions; rape crisis centers; ethnic community organizations; faith-based organizations

Department of Justice (DOJ)

Office for Victims of Crime

The U.S. Department of Justice's (USDOJ) Office of Victims of Crime (OVC) provides services for pre-certified trafficking victims (see USDOJ charts for more information). Services include housing or shelter; food; medical, mental health, and dental services; interpreter/translator services; criminal justice victim advocacy; legal services; social services advocacy; literacy education; and/or employment assistance.

See http://www.ojp.usdoj.gov/ovc/grants/traffickingmatrix.html for more information about these services. In addition, OVC's Online Directory of Crime Victim Services identifies local organizations providing services for crime victims: http://ovc.ncjrs.gov/findvictimservices/.

Certification for Foreign Victims

HHS is the Federal agency authorized to certify adult foreign victims of human trafficking, which allows them access to federally funded benefits and services to the same extent as refugees. Similarly, HHS is the Federal agency authorized to provide Eligibility Letters for foreign child victims of human trafficking, which allows them access to federally funded benefits and services to the same extent as refugees. The Office of Refugee Resettlement (ORR) within HHS issues all Certification and Eligibility Letters. Trafficking victims who are U.S. citizens or Lawful Permanent Residents (LPR) 1 do not need Certification or Letters of Eligibility to be eligible for similar benefits and services.

Steps to Obtaining Certification for Foreign Victims

According to the Trafficking Victims Protection Act of 2000 (TVPA), there are three requirements for Certification for adult victims of human trafficking:

- An individual must have been subjected to a severe form of trafficking in persons, as defined in the TVPA;
- A victim is willing to assist in every reasonable way in the investigation and prosecution of the trafficking case, or is unable to cooperate with such a request due to physical or psychological trauma; and
- The U.S. Department of Homeland Security (DHS) has granted Continued Presence (CP) to the victim, or notified the victim that his or her T-visa application is bona fide or approved.

Continued Presence

The Department of Homeland Security's Immigration and Customs Enforcement (ICE) grants Continued Presence (CP), which is a one-year form of immigration relief that Federal law enforcement officials request on behalf of a victim of a severe form of trafficking who is also a potential witness. Continued Presence allows the victim to remain in the United States during the course of an investigation or prosecution as well as obtain an

Employment Authorization Document (EAD), which provides the victim with the documentation required to work legally in the United States.

T- Visa

As previously discussed, the T-visa is a non-immigrant T-visa that allows a foreign victim of human trafficking to remain in the United States for up to four years. The victim must apply directly to DHS for T non-immigrant status by filing an application for a T-visa (also called the U.S. Citizen and Immigration Services Form I-914). Assistance from an immigration attorney or other legal service provider is often helpful in completing the application.

Since foreign trafficking victims often have complicated legal needs, it is important to connect them with an immigration attorney as soon as possible. For guidance in initiating legal assistance for victims, consult the National Human Trafficking Resource Center and/or local service providers listed in the OVC Online Directory with experience in working with trafficking victims (http://ovc.ncjrs.gov/ findvictimservices/).

As described in the U.S. Department of Homeland Security's Instructions for Completing Form I-914, a Federal law enforcement officer endorsement is strongly advised. If a victim does not submit a Federal law enforcement endorsement as a part of his or her T-visa application, then the victim must submit an explanation describing attempts to obtain the endorsement and accounting for the lack of or unavailability of the endorsement. Alternately, the victim must submit an explanation describing why he or she did not attempt to obtain the Federal law enforcement endorsement.

There are several benefits to a T visa, including:

- Legal non-immigrant T-status in the United States for a period of four years;
- Employment authorization;
- Possibility of adjusting status to Lawful Permanent Resident; and
- Immediate family members may obtain non-immigrant T-status as T-visa derivatives.

Derivative T-Visas

Family members (known as derivatives) of trafficking victims who have received a T-visa can apply for a special T-visa for derivatives. Eligible family members include the spouse, child, parent, or an unmarried minor sibling of a victim of trafficking victim who is under 21 years of age, or the spouse or child of a victim of trafficking who is 21 years of age or older. Like Certified trafficking victims, T-visa derivatives are eligible for Federal benefits and services to the same extent as refugees. Also, derivatives can apply for EADs.

After Continued Presence or a T-visa is issued

When the U.S. Department of Homeland Security grants an adult victim Continued Presence, a T visa, or notice of a bona fide T-visa application, DHS notifies the U.S. Department of Health and Human Services (HHS). HHS contacts the victim- witness coordinator, victim-witness control officer, or the immigration attorney (if any) to obtain the name of the service provider to issue the Certification Letter.

The service provider helps the victim apply for and receive the refugee benefits and services for which he or she is eligible.

The Certification Letter

The Certification Letter indicates a victim's eligibility for federally funded benefits and services. It contains a Certification date; eligibility for benefits and services begins on the date of Certification. Certification letters do not expire, but many benefits and services are time sensitive. Derivatives (family members of a victim) do not receive Certification Letters. The period of eligibility for benefits and services for T-visa derivatives begins on the date of issuance of the derivative T-visa, not on the date of issuance of the trafficking victim's T-visa or on the Certification date in the victim's Certification letter.

Temporary Assistance for Needy Families (TANF), Office of Family Assistance (OFA), Administration for Children and Families (ACF), HHS:

TANF funds State programs that provide assistance for families with children when the parents or other caretaker relatives are unable to provide for the family's basic needs. Each State and territory decides both the benefits it will provide and the eligibility criteria for receiving financial assistance payments or other types of TANF benefits and services. In order to be eligible for TANF, the client must be a member of an eligible family that also meets other TANF programmatic eligibility requirements, such as income, resources, and residency.

If a Certified adult victim (or Eligible minor) is not eligible for TANF, he or she may be eligible for ORR Refugee Cash Assistance (RCA), as long as the victim meets RCA program eligibility requirements (see the following section on ORR benefits and services). Check with your local TANF office to obtain information on eligibility for TANF assistance or other TANF benefits and services. http://www.acf.hhs.gov/programs/ofa/

Medicaid, Centers for Medicare & Medicaid Services (CMS), HHS:

Medicaid provides health coverage for low-income pregnant women, children, parents, adults, and those with disabilities who may have no insurance or inadequate medical insurance. Although the Federal Government establishes general guidelines for the program, each State establishes Medicaid program requirements. The local Medicaid office evaluates a certified adult victim for eligibility for Medicaid. If the Medicaid office determines the person is not eligible for Medicaid, then the victim may be eligible for ORR Refugee Medical Assistance (RMA), as long as the victim meets RMA program eligibility requirements (see the following section on ORR benefits and services). For specific information about enrollment in Medicaid, eligibility, coverage, and services for your State, please contact your local Medicaid office.

For additional information on Medicaid, go to: https://www.cms.hhs.gov/home/medicaid.asp

State Children's Health Insurance Program (SCHIP), CMS, HHS:

SCHIP provides health coverage for children who do not qualify for Medicaid, yet do not have private insurance. Children who do not currently have health insurance may be eligible, even if parents are working. This insurance pays for doctor visits, prescription medicines, hospitalizations, and other services. The Federal Government and individual States jointly finance SCHIP, and each State administers SCHIP. Within broad Federal guidelines, each State determines the design of its program, eligibility groups, benefit packages, payment levels for coverage, and administrative and operating procedures. States have different eligibility rules, but in most States, uninsured children 18 years old and younger, whose families earn up to $34,100 a year (for a family of four), are eligible.

https://www.cms.gov/home/chip.asp;
www.insurekidsnow.gov, 1-877-KIDS- NOW

Health Resources and Services Administration (HRSA), HHS:

HRSA offers health care and support to uninsured, underserved, and special needs populations. HRSA issues grants to federally funded health centers that are available to anyone regardless of their ability to pay. The health centers charge patients using a sliding fee scale, based on their income. Health centers provide well-care checkups, treatment for sick patients, complete care for pregnant patients, immunizations and checkups for children, dental care, prescription drugs, as well as mental health and substance abuse care. Health centers are located in most cities and many rural areas.

To find a health center, go to:
http://findahealthcenter.hrsa.gov/Search_HCC.aspx;
http://www.hrsa.gov/index.html; 1-888-ASK-HRSA

Substance Abuse and Mental Health Services Administration (SAMHSA), HHS:

SAMHSA funds services for individuals who have or are at risk for mental and substance abuse disorders. State substance abuse and mental health agencies administer these programs. All decisions regarding eligibility for services and types of treatment are made at the local and State levels or by the provider. Contact your State substance abuse and mental health agencies to find out what services are available in your area.

Substance Abuse Resources:

For a listing of State substance abuse agencies, go to: http://findtreatment.samhsa.gov/ufds/abusedirectors

To find a substance abuse and/or mental health treatment program near you, go to: http://findtreatment.samhsa.gov/

Mental Health Resources:

For a listing of State mental health agencies, go to:
http://store.samhsa.gov/mhlocator
To find a mental health treatment program near you, go to:
http://store.samhsa.gov/mhlocator

National Suicide Prevention Lifeline:

SAMHSA's Center for Mental Health Services funds a 24-hour, toll-free, suicide prevention service available to anyone in emotional distress or suicidal crisis. If your client needs help, call 1-800-273-TALK (8255). Crisis counselors will locate the closest possible crisis center in your area. With more than 130 crisis centers across the country, the Lifeline's mission is to provide immediate assistance to anyone seeking mental health services. See http://www.suicidepreventionlifeline.org/ for more information.

For additional SAMHSA substance abuse and mental health resources, go to: http://www.samhsa.gov/treatment/index.aspx or call SAMHSA's

24-Hour Toll-Free Referral Helpline at 1-800-662-HELP (1-800-662-4357).

Refugee Cash Assistance (RCA), Office of Refugee Resettlement (ORR), Administration for Children and Families (ACF), HHS:

RCA provides cash assistance for trafficking victims who are ineligible for TANF, Supplemental Security Income (SSI), Medicaid, or State Children's Health Insurance Program (SCHIP). RCA benefits are available for up to eight months from the date of Certification. Recipients of Refugee Cash Assistance are required to register for employment services and participate in employability service programs, unless specifically exempted by State criteria. Minors who cannot comply with the employability service requirements - such as minors in school or those without work authorization - cannot receive RCA. Also, a recipient of RCA cannot be a full-time student in an institution of higher education.

http://www.acf.hhs.gov/programs/orr/benefits/cma.htm

Refugee Medical Assistance (RMA), ORR, ACF, HHS:

RMA provides medical assistance for trafficking victims who are ineligible for TANF, SSI, Medicaid, or SCHIP. RMA benefits are available for up to eight months from the date of Certification, or the date of Eligibility if the client is a minor. Depending on the State, RMA may cover costs associated with a medical screening.

http://www.acf.hhs.gov/programs/orr/benefits/cma.htm

Refugee Social Services and Targeted Assistance, ORR, ACF, HHS:

These programs support employability services and other services that address participants" barriers to self-sufficiency and integration and may include employment services, employability assessment, on-the-job training, English-language training, vocational training, social adjustment services, interpretation and translation services, job-related day care for children, citizenship and naturalization services, etc. Employability services are designed to enable trafficking victims and other eligible populations to obtain employment and become self-sufficient as soon as possible. Services provided by Refugee Social Services and Targeted Assistance programs differ by State. Benefits are available for up to 60 months from the date of Certification or Eligibility. Citizenship and naturalization services and referral and interpreter services are not time limited; they may be provided beyond 60 months. Minors must have work authorization in order to benefit from employment services.

http://www.acf.hhs.gov/programs/orr/programs/ref_social_prg.htm

http://www.acf.hhs.gov/programs/orr/programs/tap.htm

Voluntary Agency Matching Grant Program, ORR, ACF, HHS:

The Voluntary Agency Matching Grant Program is an alternative to public assistance designed to enable clients to become self-sufficient within four to six months from the date of Certification or Eligibility. A network of approximately 230 local resettlement offices in 43 States provides Matching Grant services, which are provided in a comprehensive multilingual, multicultural manner. Clients must complete enrollment in Matching Grant within 31 days of the date of Certification or Eligibility. Required services are case management, maintenance assistance (cash assistance and housing, when needed), and employment services. Matching Grant can make referrals for additional services such as English-language training, social adjustment services, health and medical services, employment training/re- certification, and support services. Matching Grant enrollees can receive Refugee Medical Assistance, but they are not eligible for Refugee Cash Assistance or TANF.

http://www.acf.hhs.gov/programs/orr/programs/match_gra nt_prg.htm

Medical Screenings, Office of Refugee Resettlement (ORR), Administration for Children and Families (ACF), HHS:

Preventive health medical screenings and assessments are available to certified trafficked persons and Eligible minors for early diagnosis and treatment of illnesses that are contagious or are barriers to self- sufficiency. This usually includes screening for tuberculosis (TB), parasites, and Hepatitis BS, as well as school vaccinations. Screenings are not available in every location. To arrange for a referral for a medical screening, contact your State Refugee Coordinator or Refugee Health Coordinator via the following Web site:

http://www.acf.hhs.gov/programs/orr/partners/state_partner s.htm

Unaccompanied Refugee Minors Program (URM), ORR, ACF, HHS:

ORR's URM program can provide care to an unaccompanied child victim of trafficking who has received an Eligibility Letter and met established criteria for reclassification or designation as an unaccompanied refugee minor. The URM program provides specialized, culturally appropriate foster care or other licensed care settings according to children's individual needs. Legal responsibility is established, under State law, to ensure that there is a legal authority to act in place of the child's unavailable parent(s). Unaccompanied child trafficking victims receive the full range of assistance, care, and services that are available to other foster children in the State. Depending on their individual needs, children are placed in foster homes, group care, independent living, or residential treatment settings. Services include: indirect financial support for housing, food, clothing, and medical care; intensive case management; family reunification; independent living skills training; educational supports; English-language training; career/college counseling; mental health services; assistance adjusting immigration status; cultural activities; recreational opportunities; support for social integration; and retention of ethnic and religious heritage. To access the URM program for a child victim of trafficking who has received an Eligibility Letter, contact the ORR Child Protection Specialist at 202-205-4582. For more information on ORR's URM program, visit the following Web site:

http://www.acf.hhs.gov/programs/orr/programs/unaccompa nied_refugee_ minors.htm

Services for Survivors of Torture Program, ORR, ACF, HHS:

ORR's Services for Survivors of Torture provides rehabilitative services, including treatment for the psychological and physical effects of torture; social and legal services; and research and training for health care providers outside of treatment centers or programs. Individuals eligible for services are those who suffered torture in foreign countries and are now present in the United States regardless of their immigration status. Individuals who have suffered torture only as a result of trafficking experiences in the United States do not meet the eligibility standard for this program.

http://www.acf.hhs.gov/programs/orr/programs/services_su rvivors_torture.htm

Child Nutrition Programs, Food and Nutrition Service, USDA:

Child Nutrition programs offer nutritious meals and snacks for low-income children in schools, child care institutions, and after-school care programs.

http://www.fns.usda.gov/cnd/

Supplemental Nutrition Assistance Program (formerly call the Food Stamp Program), Food and Nutrition Service, USDA:

SNAP provides nutrition assistance to low-income individuals and families so they can buy the food needed for good health. Benefits are provided on an electronic card that is used like an ATM card at participating grocery stores.

To apply for benefits, or for information about the SNAP, contact your local SNAP office at http://www.fns.usda.gov/snap/outreach/map.htm or call your State's SNAP hotline number at http://www.fns.usda.gov/snap/outreach/map.htm.

An online Pre-Screening Tool is available at http://www.snap-step1.usda.gov/fns/ to find out if your client could be eligible prior to applying at your local office.

Special Supplemental Nutrition Program for Women, Infants and Children (WIC), Food and Nutrition Service, USDA:

WIC provides supplemental food packages for nutritionally at-risk, low-income pregnant, breastfeeding, and post-partum women; infants; and children up to five years of age. The following benefits are provided to WIC participants: supplemental nutritious foods; nutrition education and counseling at WIC clinics; and screening and referrals to other health, welfare, and social services. The following Web site has toll-free numbers for WIC State agencies:

http://www.fns.usda.gov/wic/contacts/tollfreenumbers.htm

Public Housing Program, HUD:

This program provides safe and affordable rental housing for low-income families, the elderly and persons with disability.

http://portal.hud.gov/hudportal/HUD?src=/program_offices /public_indian_ housing/programs/ph

Tenant-Based Vouchers, HUD:

Low-income housing agencies issue Housing Choice Vouchers to very low-income individuals and families, so that they can lease safe and affordable privately owned rental housing.

http://portal.hud.gov/hudportal/HUD?src=/program_offices /public_indian_ housing/programs/hcv

Victim of Crime Act (VOCA) Emergency Funds, Criminal Section, Civil Rights Division, U.S. Department of Justice (USDOJ):

VOCA emergency funds, which assist victims with emergency needs when other resources are unavailable, include crisis intervention, shelter/temporary housing, food, clothing, legal assistance, transportation costs, forensic medical examinations, emergency child care, and interpreters. Similar funds are available through the Federal Bureau of Investigation (FBI), the Executive Office for United States Attorneys at USDOJ, and Immigration and Customs Enforcement (ICE) within the U.S. Department of Homeland Security (DHS).

Victims' Rights and Services, Federal Victim-Witness Coordinators within Criminal Section of Civil Rights Division; FBI; U.S. Attorneys" Offices; and Other USDOJ Agencies:

Victim Witness staff ensure that victims of Federal crimes, regardless of age or citizenship, are afforded rights and services as set forth in the Attorney General Guidelines for Victim and Witness Assistance (May2005), including rights afforded by the Federal Crime Victims Rights Act, such as privacy and confidentiality, restitution, notification of case status, and protection against threats and intimidation. Victim Witness staff may also provide information about and referrals for direct services such as medical assistance, mental health counseling, shelter, pro bono and low-cost legal services, and other essential services.

http://www.justice.gov/olp/pdf/ag_guidelines.pdf

Emergency Witness Assistance Program (EWAP) USDOJ:

EWAP provides emergency funds to assist witnesses and potential witnesses on an emergency basis to ensure their well-being and availability for court proceedings or other activities related to ongoing civil or criminal cases. Services include relocation and moving expenses; emergency telephone service to maintain contact with the Government; temporary subsistence and housing; emergency needs (clothing, furniture) when the individual must be moved quickly; and child or senior care expenses. The Executive Office for U.S. Attorneys administers these funds. EWAP is usually limited to less than 30 days and less than $4,000.

http://www.justice.gov.oig/reports/EOUSA/e0102/index.htm

Witness Security Program, USDOJ:

The Witness Security Program provides protection and assistance to witnesses and their immediate family members before, during and after a trial. The Attorney

General determines whether a witness qualifies for the Witness Security Program, based on recommendations from U.S. Attorneys. The U.S. Marshals Service moves a witness and his or her immediate family to a secure location and typically provides them with authentic documentation to assume a new identity. In addition to providing witnesses with 24-hour protection during all court proceedings, the U.S. Marshals Service assists with housing, medical care, job training, employment and subsistence funding to cover basic living expenses until witnesses achieve self sufficiency.

http://www.usmarshals.gov/witsec/index.html

Services for Trafficking Victims Discretionary Grant, Office of Victims of Crime (OVC), USDOJ:

OVC funds services for trafficking victims prior to HHS granting a Certification Letter to the victim. Services include housing or shelter; food; medical, mental health, and dental services; interpreter/translator services; criminal justice victim advocacy; legal services; social services advocacy; literacy education; and/or employment assistance.

http://www.ojp.usdoj.gov/ovc/grants/traffickingmatrix.html

Victims of Crime Act (VOCA) Victim Assistance, VOCA Formula Grants to States, USDOJ:

OVC provides formula grant funding to the States to support local victim assistance programs that provide direct services to victims. Typically the State awards sub-grants to victim assistance programs to provide specialized services at the community level. Some victim assistance providers serve all crime victims; others may limit services to a specific type of victimization, such as child abuse, sexual assault, or domestic violence. While there are few VOCA-supported programs that are dedicated solely to serving human trafficking victims, many programs, such as rape crisis centers and domestic violence shelters, do provide services to human trafficking victims.

http://www.ojp.usdoj.gov/ovc/publications/factshts/cvf2010/intro.html

Department of State (DOS):

DOS represents the United States in the global fight to combat human trafficking by engaging with foreign governments, international and inter-governmental organizations, and civil society to develop and implement effective strategies for confronting this form of modern slavery. This occurs through bilateral and multilateral diplomacy, targeted foreign assistance, public outreach, and specific projects on trafficking in persons. The Department chairs the PITF and SPOG, as described above.

The Office to Monitor and Combat Trafficking in Persons (G/TIP) produces the annual *Trafficking in Persons Report*, which assesses the strengths and weaknesses of foreign governments' efforts to address human trafficking and serves as the U.S. government's principal diplomatic tool to promote anti-trafficking reforms. The Report also spotlights the forms that modern slavery takes around the world and encourages partnerships with civil society. G/TIP funds international anti-trafficking programs, taking into account the assessments of individual countries as set out in the annual TIP Report.

The Bureau of Population, Refugees, and Migration (PRM) funds international anti-trafficking programs, as well as the *Return, Reintegration, and Family Reunification Program for Victims of Trafficking.*

In addition, global programs funded by the **Bureau of Democracy, Human Rights, and Labor** (DRL) promote worker rights and address labor violations, including trafficking in persons.

The Department's security and law enforcement arm, the **Bureau of Diplomatic Security** plays an essential role investigating human trafficking crimes in collaboration with other law enforcement entities.

The **Office of Global Women's Issues (GWI)** led by Ambassador-at-Large Melanne Verveer, works for the political, economic, and social empowerment of women. Integral to this work is a focus on responding to and preventing violence against women, which contributes to efforts to prevent human trafficking. The Department's consular officers also have an important role and are trained in combating trafficking in persons at U.S.

embassies and consulates worldwide, in particular in issuing employment or education-based nonimmigrant visas.

Department of Homeland Security (DHS):

DHS consists of more than 20 component agencies and offices, including both law enforcement entities and the nation's immigration services. In 2010, DHS launched the Blue Campaign – a first-of-its-kind campaign to coordinate and enhance the Department's anti-human trafficking efforts. *The Blue Campaign*—which includes 17 DHS components, such as U.S. Immigration and Customs Enforcement, U.S. Citizenship and Immigration Services, U.S. Customs and Border Protection, the U.S. Coast Guard, and the Federal Law Enforcement Training Center— harnesses and leverages the varied authorities and resources of the Department to deter human trafficking by increasing awareness, protecting victims, and contributing to a robust criminal justice response.

As the largest investigative agency within DHS, **U.S. Immigration and Customs Enforcement**

(ICE)/Homeland Security Investigations (HSI) conducts domestic and international investigations of human trafficking, child sex tourism, and forced child labor. Since the passage of the PROTECT Act of 2003, HIS has focused investigative resources on investigating U.S. citizens and lawful permanent residents that travel abroad to engage in illicit sexual activity with minors. Worldwide, HIS conducts law enforcement training and public awareness campaigns, such as *Hidden in Plain Sight*, as part of its outreach efforts. HSI also provides trafficking victims with short-term immigration relief, manages the HIS Victim Assistance Program, and operates a 24-hour hotline to report potential trafficking activity at 1-866-DHS-2-ICE.

U.S. Citizenship and Immigration Services (USCIS) grants immigration relief to trafficking victims, while also conducting training for non-governmental organizations and law enforcement. USCIS officers are trained to identify potential trafficking victims and to notify law enforcement personnel upon encountering such individuals.

U.S. Customs and Border Protection (CBP) conducts public campaigns, such as *No Te Engañes*, to raise awareness among potential victims and vulnerable communities. CBP also screens unaccompanied alien children to identify human trafficking victims.

.

The U.S. Coast Guard routinely conducts maritime operations independently and with other federal law enforcement agencies and international partners to combat illegal migration, including human trafficking.

The Federal Law Enforcement Training Center offers human trafficking training to federal, state, local, campus, and tribal law enforcement officers throughout the United States.

Additionally, human trafficking courses are delivered at several of the **International Law Enforcement Academies** including the academy in Gaborone, Botswana, which is managed by the **Federal Law Enforcement Training Center**. DHS is the chair of the *Human Smuggling and Trafficking Center* steering group in coordination with the Department of Justice and Department of State. The Center provides a mechanism to bring together federal agency representatives from the policy, law enforcement, intelligence, and diplomatic areas to work together on a full time basis to achieve increased effectiveness, and to convert intelligence into effective law enforcement and other action. For more information, please visit the DHS Blue Campaign webpage or the DHS Blue Campaign Facebook page.

Department of Defense (DOD):

DOD endeavors to ensure that the U.S. military, its civilian employees, and its contractors are aware of and adopt the zero tolerance policy on human trafficking. A demand reduction campaign helps make contractors, government personnel, and military members aware of common signs of human trafficking and provides a hotline number to report suspected incidents. The awareness campaign is reinforced by the requirement for all military and civilian members of the Department to take annual trafficking awareness training. DOD's subordinate organizations are further required to report on completion of their personnel's annual training. Public service announcements on labor and sex trafficking are in effect. DOD routinely holds conferences and workshops to further educate personnel and explore innovative measures to combat TIP.

Department of Justice (DOJ):

The Human Trafficking Prosecution Unit, a specialized anti-trafficking unit of DOJ's **Civil Rights Division's Criminal Section** prosecutes traffickers in partnership with **U.S. Attorney's Offices** nationwide. The cases are investigated by the **Federal Bureau of Investigation** or the **Department of Homeland Security's Immigration and Customs Enforcement** as well as other federal, state, and local law enforcement agencies. Its national complaint line is 1-888-428-7581.

The Criminal Division's **Child Exploitation and Obscenity Section** prosecutes cases of child sex trafficking and child sex tourism.

Federal Bureau of Investigation – Innocence Lost Child Prostitution Task Forces and Working Groups: Nationwide, there are several taskforces and working groups that work in conjunction with local law enforcement to combat Child Position or the Commercial Sexual Exploitation of Children (CSEC).

The Criminal Division's **Overseas Prosecutorial**

Development, Assistance and Training Program provide anti-trafficking training and technical assistance to law enforcement internationally.

The **Bureau of Justice Assistance** funds 38 anti-trafficking task forces comprised of local, state, and federal law enforcement as well as non-governmental victim service providers.

The **Office of Victims of Crime** funds nongovernmental organizations to provide services to U.S. citizen victims and foreign victims prior to certification by the **Department of Health and Human Services**. Significant research is conducted by the **National Institute of Justice** and the **Bureau of Justice Statistics**. DOJ also produces the *Attorney General's Annual Report* to Congress on *U.S. Government Activities to Combat Trafficking in Persons*.

Department of Agriculture (USDA):

The USDA established a **Consultative Group to Eliminate the Use of Child Labor and Forced Labor in Imported Agricultural Products** pursuant to Section 3205 of the Food, Conservation, and Energy Act of 2008. The group represents a diverse set of government, private sector, academic and non-governmental organization (NGO) entities, and has been charged with developing and making recommendations to the **Secretary of Agriculture** regarding guidelines to reduce the likelihood that agricultural products imported into the United States are produced with the use of child or forced labor. Within one year after receiving these recommendations, the Secretary is required to finalize the guidelines and release them for public comment.

Department of Labor (DOL):

DOL's **Wage and Hour Division (WHD)** carries out civil law enforcement in the nation's workplaces and its field investigators are often the first government authorities to detect exploitive labor practices. WHD coordinates with other law enforcement agencies to ensure restitution on behalf of victims of trafficking. To enhance this coordination, WHD is part of the **Anti-Human Trafficking Coordination Team** (ATC Team) pilot program that is being developed by the **Federal Enforcement Working Group** on trafficking (headed by the Department of Justice). WHD has responsibility for certifying U-Visas per the TVPA and has established protocols for certification based on five qualifying criminal activities– involuntary servitude, peonage, trafficking, obstruction of justice and witness tampering –when it detects them in the process of investigating a violation of an employment law under its jurisdiction, such as minimum wage or overtime.

DOL's **Employment and Training Administration** offers job search, placement and counseling services, and vocational skills training to trafficking victims.

Additionally, DOL's **Bureau of International Labor Affairs** (ILAB) awards grants to implement programs to combat exploitive child labor around the globe. Many of these programs have direct service, awareness, and policy activities to address child trafficking as one of the worst forms of child labor.

ILAB publishes three reports on child labor and/or forced labor in countries worldwide, including the *"List of Goods Produced by Child or Forced Labor"* required by the Trafficking Victims Protection Reauthorization Act of 2005 (TVPRA list), which informs the public about 128 goods from 70 countries that DOL has reason to believe are produced by forced labor, child labor, or both in violation of international standards. DOL uses the TVPRA list and other reports as tools to communicate the urgent need for effective action by governments, private sectors, and others to address these problems.

Department of Health and Human Services (HHS):

HHS leads the **Rescue & Restore Victims of Human Trafficking** public awareness campaign, funds organizations to conduct outreach to foreign and U.S. citizen victims, funds comprehensive case management and support services for foreign victims in the United States, and certifies foreign victims of a severe form of trafficking in persons to be eligible to receive Federal benefits and services to the same extent as refugees. A range of programs also assist youth at-risk of trafficking, including the *Runaway and Homeless Youth Program.*

HHS also funds the **National Human Trafficking Resource Center** that provides a nationwide 24/7 hotline at 1-888-3737-888.

Department of Education (ED):

ED's Office of Safe and Drug-Free Schools uses the Web, list serves, and trainings to raise awareness both to prevent trafficking of children and to increase victim identification of trafficked children in schools. Trafficking often involves school-age children—particularly those not living with their parents—who are vulnerable to coerced labor exploitation, domestic servitude, or commercial sexual exploitation. Traffickers target minor victims through telephone chat-lines, social networking websites, on the streets, in malls, as well as by using girls to recruit other girls at school and in after-school programs.

The Office of Safe and Drug-Free Schools develops and disseminates materials about preventing human trafficking, such as *"Human Trafficking of Children in the United States: A Fact Sheet for Schools."*

The **Office of Safe and Drug-Free Schools** develops and disseminates materials about preventing human trafficking, such as *Human Trafficking of Children in the United States: A Fact Sheet for Schools* and the *Readiness and Emergency Management for Schools Web site.*

Agency for International Development (USAID):

USAID funds international programs that prevent trafficking, protect and assist victims, and support prosecutions through training for police and criminal justice personnel. USAID reinforces successful anti-trafficking initiatives by funding programs that support economic development, child protection, women's empowerment, good governance, education, health, and human rights. USAID supports individual country assessments of the scope and nature of trafficking and the efforts of government, civil society, and international organization to combat it.

U.S. Equal Employment Opportunity Commission (EEOC or Commission):

The EEOC investigates, attempts to informally resolve, and litigates charges alleging discrimination on the basis of race, color, national origin, sex, religion, age, disability, and genetic information. Inappropriate cases, therefore, the EEOC is able to secure civil remedies (e.g., monetary and equitable relief) for trafficking victims. In 2010, the EEOC participated for the first time in both the PITF and SPOG meetings as a full partner. On January 19, 2011, the Commission conducted a public meeting on the *Agency's Role in Fighting Human Trafficking and Forced Labor*. The EEOC has committed to active participation in order to identify additional labor trafficking cases through its 53 offices nationwide.

CHAPTER 7

COMMUNICATING WITH VICTIMS OF HUMAN TRAFFICKING

In order to transition a victim of human trafficking from a victim to a witness, there are some points to consider and key messages you should convey. Effective communication is essential in gaining trust of victims as well as defining their immediate needs. Effective witness management extends into the courtroom when the time comes to present testimony and evidence to a jury. First and foremost, you will need to keep in mind that most victims fear deportation. Once it is revealed they do not have their legal identification, they will expect you to charge them as illegal immigrants and have them deported back to their country of origin. While many of these victims are women and children who have been raped or beaten, their current situation may actually be better than where they came from. Therefore, it will be important for you to convey to the victim that they are safe and that they will not be deported.

Other common fears and beliefs experienced by victims of human trafficking may include:

Fear of reprisal against the victim or their family by employers, traffickers, pimps, law enforcement officers, and government officials.

Many trafficking victims have expressed fear of being returned to their environment or traffickers. Those who maintain control of trafficking victims do so in a variety of means including intimidation and physical punishment. They often fear being returned to the traffickers and experiencing beatings, rape, or confinement for leaving, disobeying or cooperating with law enforcement. The victim may have observed these "lessons" being inflicted on other victims for minor transgressions and believe the same will happen to them if they are returned. It is extremely common for traffickers and their associates to use threats against a victim's family, especially minor children, to manipulate and control them.

Fear of shame and rejection, or even punishment by the victim's family members or members of their community.

Human trafficking victims may not only be afraid for their families but also worry about how their parents, husbands, or others will react if they find out the victim had worked as a prostitute or had been sexually abused. In some countries and cultures it is not uncommon for parents, siblings, or spouses to blame, physically punish, or banish the victim for what has happened to them. Revelation of what has happened to a victim can cause irreparable damage to relationships with their family leaving them with no support network. Some trafficking victims may also be worried their family members will discover they have not earned anticipated or expected income or that they fled without repaying a debt.

Identification by law enforcement authorities.

A large percentage of human trafficking victims have travelled into the destination country illegally. Additionally, many have had their identification documents confiscated by traffickers and are uncertain of their legal status in the destination country. Many foreign born victims have experience with corrupt authorities at home which fosters mistrust or the police and other officials. It is not uncommon in some countries where officials are actually complicit in the human trafficking organization or take advantage of victims by using their powers to arrest and subsequently robbing the victims of their money. In some cases corrupt officials have even resold/re-trafficked the women. Traffickers take advantage of these experiences by instilling fear of law enforcement and government officials by telling the victims they will be imprisoned, physically harmed, prevented from ever returning home, or be returned home against their will.

Reprisal by home country authorities.

As noted above, government and law enforcement officials from a victim's home country may be complicit in the trafficking process. Victims may fear those corrupt officials will retaliate against them or their family, whether or not they are returned.

Betrayal by fellow victims, co-workers, co-residents, or community members.

Experience has shown that it is not safe to assume that victims in the same location or situation, or even those from the same region or country, trust each other. Although victims in from the same living or working environment can form strong bonds there are also instances where victims harbor resentment, benefit financially, earn respect or extra privileges by disclosing information about other victims. There are also cases where victims remain connected to traffickers to whom they pass information about other victims.

Loyalty to and dependence on traffickers, employers, pimps or others in the network.

Some victims may have romantic relationships with those involved in the trafficking network. To an observer, these relationships may appear inexplicable unless one considers the systematic isolation and dependency that are major components of the coercion used by perpetrators. In many instances cruel or violent acts against the victim are alternated with gestures of mercy and kindness. A victim may come to believe they are being taken care of and the manipulation causes the victim to believe that the best hope for his/her future lies in the hands of those who are simultaneously abusing and exploiting them.

Failing to recognize themselves as victims.

Many victims of trafficking do not self-identify themselves as victims. They assume what they are doing is just a way of life, a way to make a living. They don't know that what has been done to them is illegal. Victims may project a sense of fear or distrust towards law enforcement, which could originate from the negative perceptions of law enforcement in their countries of origin. It's critical to convey that you can protect them and help them to obtain the assistance they need. Most victims will generally be unaware of any rights they may have. From their perspective, they may not think they even have the right to live. Therefore, it's important for you to tell them they do have rights and that they may be entitled to receive benefits and services to rebuild their lives.

Working with an Interpreter

Many human trafficking victims do not speak English and are unfamiliar with U.S. culture. A critical component in transitioning a victim into a witness is to make every reasonable effort the insure communications are in their native language. Using a translator can be a cumbersome process but it allows the victim to convey information in their native language and allows them to begin accessing and environment outside of that involving the trafficker and/or other victims.

Take into consideration a victim's cultural and social background as these traits will impact the way victims should be managed as witnesses, as well as the way the investigation of their cases are carried out. If possible, you should work with a culturally and linguistically competent. Ideally, this person could serve as a language interpreter and be able to interpret the cultural values and unique behaviors that are characteristic of the victim's national and ethnic background.

Caution should be exercised when selecting and working with interpreters as they may pose a risk to the victim if they do not understand the dangers associated with breaches or security or confidentiality. Interpreters should be screened to ensure they do not know the victim, the trafficker, their families, and do not otherwise have a conflict of interest.

Several factors about the interpreter should be taken into account during the selection process, including: age, gender, general translation experience, experience with the field you are working in, cultural background, and potential connection with the survivor or trafficker. Interpreters may be used as both language translators and culture brokers. They should be able to translate the nuances and meanings of language, versus simply a literal translation. On the other hand, they should be instructed to completely translate all communication. Be aware of cultural differences in material that is deemed "acceptable" to discuss. For instance, some translators may avoid material that is sexual in nature, due to cultural taboos.

Be cautious about selecting a translator who may have connections to the trafficker or their associates. Interpreters and interviewers who speak the same language may make the victim feel more comfortable and help to build trust. However, this can also cause the opposite effect. Victims may not trust, or feel embarrassed speaking to someone from their community or same cultural background about taboo topics such as prostitution or sexual abuse.

It is recommended that attempts be made to work with an interpreter or individual from a local organization familiar with working with victims who have experienced sexual violence and an individual who is not from her home community, unless the victim indicates otherwise.

Depending on the resources of the investigating agency and the local protocols about using court certified translators it might be advantageous to use a trusted friend or colleague to assist with communicating with the victim.

Don't utilize an interpreter or individual who might judgmental, shocked, or offended by the information the victim reveals. It is not uncommon for victims of human sexual trafficking to have experienced severe and graphic abuse at the hands of their traffickers. Interpreters should be fully briefed about the subject of trafficking and the range of physical and sexual abuse that often accompanies it.

Interview Considerations – the Victim's Situation

An interview with a trafficking victim may take place while he/she is still in a trafficking situation, when he/she is in the care of a service organization, or once they have moved beyond the trafficking situation, either on their own or through law enforcement intervention.

Be prepared to believe the victim until the investigation shows otherwise, remembering that truth is stranger than fiction. In several sex trafficking cases, the first-responding officers stated that their initial reaction was disbelief, not necessarily of the victim herself but of the facts she related. For example, in one case, a victim described initiation "parties" in which victims were held down and repeatedly raped by a series of men with the goal of bringing as many men to ejaculation as possible. In another case, victims described being forced to lay naked on a bed while 20 or more men entered the room in approximately 10-minute intervals and penetrated them.

In a third case, young middle-class college women described being forced to engage in sex in the backrooms of popular nightclubs in a particular jurisdiction. In each case, the first-responding officer described being suspicious because the statements seemed outlandish. Each of these cases resulted in the prosecution and conviction of a sex trafficker.

Some important considerations while interviewing those who are still in a trafficking situation is that victims often:

- Fear of reprisal from those involved with or associated with the traffickers. Many traffickers maintain control over a victim via intimidation and physical punishments such as beatings, rape, and confinement.

- Fell trapped with no safe way out of their current situation

- Are working or have worked in an often illegal situation such as prostitution

- May be residing illegal in the country to which they were trafficked

- Have little or no knowledge of their legal rights and options

- Have experienced limited personal freedoms

- Are likely to have experience sexual, physical, and/or psychological abuse and threats against themselves or their family

- May lie about their age or background, especially if they are minors or runaways

- May be trapped in situations of debt bondage or other financial obligations

- Might have been trafficked by organized crime with links to corrupt government officials or members of the police or military in their home country

- Face ethnic, social and gender discrimination in their current environment or in their country of origin

- Frequently adopt self-protective measures of demonstrate symptoms of post traumatic stress demonstrated by impaired sense of time or space, memory loss of certain events or circumstances, or engaging in risky or self destructive behaviors

Those who have left the trafficking situation, either of their own accord or through intervention often:

- Have many of the same concerns identified with those currently in a trafficking situation (see above)
- Continue to feel, and may be, watched or under surveillance by traffickers or others associated with the traffickers
- Have outstanding debts owed to the traffickers by them or their family
- Remain vulnerable to retribution or threats of retribution again themselves and/or their families
- May only have temporary or no residency status in a destination country

- Feel they are socially stigmatized by their experience and their work and risk rejection by their family and community if their past activities are revealed

Special Considerations

It should not always be assumed that all trafficking victims are traumatized, consider themselves victims, despise or loathe their captors, or even wish to escape or go home. It is not uncommon for female trafficking victims to have an intimate relationship with someone involved in the trafficking network. It is also not uncommon for a victim to feel loyalty, gratitude, or dependence on someone involved in the victim's situation. Some victims do not perceive themselves as having been the victims of human trafficking according to legal definitions and do not want to be treated as victims. They may regard their experience as the result of a poor decision for which they are obligated to fulfill.

Some victims may view their circumstance as only a temporary situation during which time they intend to pay off a debt and support their family. Unfortunately, some victims believe their current situation is better than the one they left and may not perceive their work situation as abusive but rather normal or expected.

Most victims are afraid and initially hesitant to cooperate, often fearing for their lives. An effective method for obtaining cooperation of a victim of human trafficking is to put their needs first. A successful investigation and prosecution of a human trafficking case is victim-centered. This requires lending support to traumatized and confused victims before you can gain their confidence. Although capturing and convicting the trafficker are top priorities, it is more strategic to put the safety, education and concerns of the victims first throughout the case investigation and prosecution.

The strategic use of words and phrases can help reassure the victim. Some examples include:

- You are safe now.
- No one here will hurt you.
- Under the Trafficking Victims Protection Act of 2000, victims of trafficking can apply for special visas or could receive other forms of immigration relief.

- Coming to us/Working with us will help you.
- You are a victim, not a criminal.
- What happened to you was wrong, and the person who did this to you should be in jail.
- You have a right to live without being abused.
- You deserve the chance to become self-sufficient and independent.
- By helping us, you are helping yourself.
- We can help get you what you need.
- We can help to protect your family.
- You can trust me.
- We want to make sure what happened to you doesn't happen to anyone else.
- You have rights.
- You are entitled to assistance. We can help you get assistance.
- If you are a victim of trafficking, you can receive help to rebuild your life safely in this country.

These communication tips will help you gain the trust of the victim and will help with the transition from victim to witness.

Generally, the victim will have four areas where their needs should be met. First is immediate assistance with housing, food, medical attention, and providing for the victim's safety and security. Second, most victims will also need mental health assistance and counseling. Third, victims need income assistance in order to help realize that he/she does not need to rely on the trafficker for sustenance. Fourth, many victim will require assistance with immigration status.

Attempt to Avoid Re-Traumatizing a Female Victim

Asking a victim to relate experiences which were frightening, humiliating, or painful can cause extreme anxiety. Many women feel ashamed of what they have done or what has happened to them. Anxiety may manifest during an interview but might manifest before or after. For many victims the anticipation of an interview is stressful. The victim might also review and regret statements they made during the interview.

In an attempt to reduce anxiety during the interview, investigators should attempt to avoid questions designed to elicit a strong or emotional reaction. Balance should be sought when asking questions that will cause distress or force her to reveal traumatic details while at the same time eliciting the details needed to prove specific elements of a crime. Care should be taken to avoid question which insinuate negative judgments about a victim's decision or actions such as "Why didn't you just leave?" or "Why did you agree to do_____?"

It is likely that many women will experience some level of anxiety, stress, or discomfort while discussing certain issues. Yet, for some it can also be therapeutic to discuss these issues and to be listened to. Avoid interrupting a victim's answer or story before she has had a chance to complete her thoughts. Try to ask questions in a supportive, non-judgmental manner.

Be aware that it can be upsetting for many female trafficking victims who are from home to speak about their children. This can be especially true for those who have not seen their children in a long time and are not sure if or when they will ever see them again.

Be prepared for physical manifestations of stress or anxiety such as crying uncontrollably, trembling or shaking, headaches, dizziness, nausea, shortness of breath or difficulty breathing, or the sudden appearance of a rash or becoming flushed. If the victim experiences these symptoms it may be best to ask the victim if she wishes to continue or attempt to re-direct questioning to another area. It may also be necessary to pause, take a break, or suspend the interview to another time.

Allow the victim to direct the pace and direction of the interview with open ended questions. Non-verbal and oral responses should be empathetic, non judgmental, and supportive. Interviewers should show concern for the victim and remind her of her strength and intelligence for having survived her ordeal. Reaffirming statements such as "You are safe now" and "No one here will hurt you" can help fortify the victim during questioning, as well as, help her cope with the aftermath.

Understanding that victims will likely fear law enforcement, law enforcement officers need to remember that a victim's first contact with a law enforcement official will be influenced by personal experiences, any unique cultural responses to law enforcement, and the conditioning for that contact imposed and reinforced by the perpetrator.

If first impressions are truly the impressions that last longest, then it is a paramount consideration for law enforcement officials in their contact with victims of human trafficking. Any approach to the victim should be a gradual and non-threatening process.

It is necessary to interview each person alone, but it is helpful to observe reactions when victims and unidentified suspects are in a group in order to carefully sort out the victims, the key perpetrators, and the enforcers.

The screening interview should take place in a comfortable environment and be conducted by someone who was not directly involved with the victim in the raids or arrest.

Cultural and language needs must be ascertained and reasonably accommodated to avoid shut down due to culturally offensive or inappropriate approaches. An arresting officer should not serve as an interpreter because the victim might be reluctant to disclose any information.

Follow sound practices in interviewing victims:

- Do not use interrogation methods.

- Be sure the victim has some control in the situation (breaks, water, seating placement).

- Due to fear and possible trauma on the part of victims, it is best to use a conversational approach rather than a rapid series of questions in order to obtain preliminary information. Victims need to feel safe at all times.

- It can be very helpful to have trusted victim service providers conduct a parallel interview as they can assist in reducing the victim's fear of law enforcement. They will not be gathering the facts of the crime, but will be assessing practical needs of the victim.

- Remember that open-ended questions will elicit more information from victims than those answerable with a yes or no.

- Beware of cultural considerations of gender, subject matter, and narrative style. Some cultures reveal a story in a circular rather than linear manner, and law enforcement must exercise patience and understanding.

- Refrain from physical contact with victims.
- It will take time and trust to elicit the facts of a case.

The effects of trauma can influence behavior of a victim during an interview. Memory loss, lack of focus, emotional reactivity, and multiple versions of a story can all be signs of trauma exhibited during interviews. Interviewers should be familiar with the signs of trauma and not assume the victim is evading the truth.

Special procedures must be used following a planned raid/rescue. It is a best practice that service providers not be present at the time of enforcement, but that they be brought in soon afterward to help stabilize victims and assess needs.

The unfortunate reality is that the perpetrator often has a significant control advantage over the victim, even when the victim has been removed to a place of safety. The perpetrator knows what conditioning techniques were used against the victim, knows the victim's weaknesses, and could have spent enough time with the victim for a measure of traumatic bonding to have affected the victim.

Victims have been dependent on traffickers and may have had a personal or romantic relationship. This is a difficult bond to break and all responders need to understand this dynamic.

The perpetrator may try to intervene or contact the victim. Following arrests, perpetrators have swiftly intervened to bail victims out of law enforcement custody or bring in attorneys as representatives of the victims. In such cases, the victims will have been coached to anticipate the arrival of attorneys, and their cooperation with law enforcement may be delayed or nonexistent. In other instances, trafficker accomplices who are known to the victim may be posing as victims.

CHAPTER 8

INTERVIEW CHECKLISTS

General Considerations

There should be a complete physical description of each identified and unidentified suspect including vehicle descriptions and any involved businesses or residences.

It is important to determine detailed information regarding the interior of any location and vehicle associated with the crime. Descriptions of entrances, locks, fortifications, interior furnishings, decorations, ornamentations, pictures, or any other unique features of the premises may prove to be important later.

Human trafficking victims rarely know the license plate numbers of vehicles they have been transported in so it may be useful to obtain detailed descriptions of the condition of the interior and exterior of any involved vehicles including damage, window or bumper stickers, seat covers, or ornaments or decorations displayed from the rear view mirror.

Don't forget to ask a human trafficking victim if he/she retained any documentary evidence such as copies of advertisements or receipts. These documents should be seized as evidence and described in detail during the interview process.

Trafficking victims should also be asked if they kept any letters they wrote or received and whether or not they kept of diary of their experiences. These records can include a detailed account of the money they have earned in prostitution or forced labor and other evidentiary data. Approach this area with sensitivity and respect because if these items do exist they may contain intimate and other material the victim considers embarrassing.

The following checklist details are some examples of questions to be asked during the interview process. While not all inclusive, they serve as a guideline for obtaining relevant information which can be used in the investigation and prosecution of human trafficking and related crimes.

Questions Pertaining to Sexual, Psychological, and Physical Abuse

Abduction-Related Questions:

- Where, when and how were you abducted/kidnapped?
- Was violence used or threatened? If so, how was it inflicted, and what were victim's injuries?
- Were weapons used? If so, obtain full description.
- Were restraints used? If so what type and how were they applied?
- Was the victim drugged in any way? If so, obtain details such as method of administration— injection, liquid, inhalation?
- Was the victim told of the consequences if he/she tried to escape? If so, obtain full details concerning the nature of the threat and who issued it.
- Was anything said? If so, what was said, by whom, and in what language, dialect or accent? Any

names or nicknames used?

- If the victim knows, where he/she was taken to and how was he/she taken there? How long did it take to travel from the abduction point to the detention point?
- Obtain full description of the place of detention; surroundings, could the victim hear voices or noises such as nearby trains or aircraft; any other details to identify the location?
- As stated above, obtain full detailed descriptions of the suspects, vehicles and premises.

Unlawful imprisonment

- Obtain full descriptions of suspects etc.
- Where was the victim kept and for how long?
- Obtain full description of the interior and surrounding areas of the location.
- How was the victim imprisoned? Was he/she physically restrained, and if so, obtain details of restraints, locks, means of access and egress, keys and who had them.
- If the victim was guarded, obtain full description of the guards and any conversations that took place.

- What was the extent of the imprisonment? Was the victim confined in one space or could he/she move around freely within a specified area?
- Was the victim told of the consequences for him/her if they tried to escape? If so, obtain full details of the nature of the threat and who issued it.
- In relation to the above points, were there any witnesses to any of the events? If so, obtain full details.

Physical and Sexual Assault

- When did the abuse take place? On how many occasions were you abused? Achieve exact dates, if possible; use significant events to set the timing if exact dates cannot be ascertained (very often the victim will report that the abuse was so frequent, even daily, that single events blur in to one).
- Where did it take place? Obtain full description of the venues as outlined above: layout of the room, bed, sofa, furnishings; ornaments; clothing worn and/or damaged; bedding, sheets, duvet, color, type.
- What was the exact nature and extent of the

assault? Obtain full description of the injuries caused: Was the sexual assault vaginal or anal rape or forced oral or manual indecent assault? Obtain exact description of the state of penile erection, of the extent of penetration and whether ejaculation took place. Were condoms used? Were any weapons or other implements used?

- What was said to the victim during the abuse or threatened violence, and by whom?

- What was the context of the abuse—was it for sexual gratification or was the victim physically or sexually assaulted in order to intimidate, coerce or train him/her? Was it punishment because he/she had disobeyed instructions or attempted to escape?

- Did the victim demonstrate physically or verbally his/her refusal or lack of consent, and if so, exactly how did he/she do so? Did he/she inflict any injuries on his/her abuser during the assault? If so, describe the injury.

- With sexual assaults, trafficked victims often report that they neither said nor did anything to resist and that they simply submitted to the abuse in order to avoid a physical assault in addition to the sexual one. It is vitally important to record this condition, not only because the assault can amount to rape not withstanding that refusal or lack of consent was not demonstrated, but because it illustrates the complete subjugation and enslavement of the victim.

- What was victim's physical condition afterwards, e.g. concussion, continuous internal or external bleeding, vomiting and nausea, etc.?

- Did the victim tell any other person about what had happened to him/her? If so, obtain the full details of that person and what was said.

- Did the victim require or receive any medical treatment for his/her injuries? If so, obtain details of doctor, hospital clinic, record made, etc.

- What was victim's state of mind and fear, both at the time and afterwards?

- What was said or done afterwards? Was the victim threatened with further abuse and, if so, in what context? Did his/her abuser(s) express regret?

- Obtain exact physical description of the attacker; any physical particularities such as tattoos, pierced ears, scars or marks, genital description and particularities, distinguishing voice, language, or accent, odor or perfume, the condition of his teeth and nails, etc.

- Were there any witnesses to any of the events? If so, obtain full details.

Trafficking Networks and the Commercial Process

In most cases, those performing the initial interview or investigation are not from the agency which will eventually prosecute the crime. There are likely also a number of other law enforcement and intelligence organizations which may have an interest in the information provided by a human trafficking victim for other larger scale investigations. Victims sometimes return to their trafficker of their own accord, return to their home countries, or stop cooperating with prosecutors. The initial interviews may provide the only opportunity to obtain information regarding the larger trafficking organization.

Recruitment

- Was the victim abducted? Or, was the initial contact between victim and trafficker voluntary? If so, who initiated the contact?

- If not voluntary, what were the means of coercion? Was the victim threatened or assaulted?

- What were the arrangements, and what did the victim understand the arrangements to mean? Did the victim know what he/she was going to be involved in?

- In case of sexual exploitation, was the victim aware that prostitution was intended, and if so, what form of prostitution was discussed—was it street walking, within brothels or call girl/escort agencies?

- Was the victim deceived as to the real purpose for being taken from the origin to the destination? If so, what was he/she told he/she was going to do (legitimate employment such as office work, work peripheral to the sex industry such as lap-dancing or hostess work, etc)?

- Did the victim sign a contract? If so, what were the terms of the contract?

- Where in the destination country was the victim told he/she was going to live and with whom?
- Did the traffickers know the victim's home address or any details of his/her family or other loved ones? Did they claim to know such details before he/she was trafficked?
- Did members of victim's family or other loved ones know of the arrangements?
- Was the victim sexually, physically or psychologically abused, or unlawfully imprisoned before he/she was trafficked? If so, obtain full details on the sexual, physical and psychological abuse.
- In relation to all of the above points, were there any witnesses to any of the events? If so, obtain full details.
- What is the age of the victim, and was his/her exploiter aware of this fact?
- Obtain full descriptions of each of the suspects in the recruitment phase.

Advertising (Origin Locations)

"Formal" Advertising

- Did the victim respond to an advertisement?

- Where did the victim see the advertisement—was it in a newspaper, magazine, contact directory, professional publication?

- If so, which one, and was it published locally or nationally? In which section did it appear—the personal columns, job vacancies, etc?

- Was it a radio or television advertisement—if so, what was the channel, etc.?

- What was the exact wording of the advertisement—what was it offering and did it name a specific individual to contact?

- What did it relate to? (Well-paid foreign work, bridal or escort agencies? etc.)

- How was contact with the advertiser to be made? Was it by personal visit, telephone, fax, e-mail or correspondence to an address or accommodation address such as a P.O. Box? If so, what were the numbers and details, etc?

- Did the victim keep a copy of the advertisement? If

so, where is it?

- Is the victim aware of anyone else who responded to the advertisement?

"Informal" Advertising

- Who told you about the "work?"
- How do you know them?
- Who introduced you to them?
- What exactly did they say?
- How did you meet them?
- Where did you meet them?
- Did they tell anyone else?
- Do you know who their friends, work colleagues, family, etc. are?
- Who have you seen them with? Can you describe them?

Premises (Origin Locations)

- Can the victim describe the conditions in which he/she was kept?
- Where the victim was detained—full

description of the premises, furnishings, etc?

- If the victim was abducted, does he/she know where he/she was kept and can he/she describe the location and/or peripheral topographical features?

- Did the recruitment involve a visit to an office or agency premises? If so, obtain a full description.

- Was contact made by a recruiting agent in a bar or nightclub? If so, obtain a full description of the suspect and the premises.

- Was the victim taken to and/or kept at any private addresses prior to leaving his/her country?

Communications (Origin Locations)

- How was contact made between the victim and the traffickers: postal service, P.O. Boxes, landline phone, mobile phone, fax, or e-mail?

- What were the numbers and/or addresses?

- Did the victim see any billing, and if so, what was the name of the subscriber?

- If it was a mobile phone, what was the make and

does the victim know the network provider; did he/she ever see it displayed on the phone screen?

- Did the trafficker use a laptop computer or personal organizer? If so, what model were they, and did the victim know any details such as access codes, e-mail service providers, etc?

Transport (Origin Locations)

- Was the victim taken out of the country covertly or overtly?
- If covertly, by what means: road, rail, ferry? Give descriptions.
- If known, what was the exact date and point of departure and where was the border crossed?
- What identity documents did the victim have and in what name and nationality? How did he/she get the documents?
- Did the victim travel alone, or was he/she accompanied by other victims and/or traffickers?
- If the victim travelled overtly, what identity documents were used? Were they genuine or

forged?

- If forged, what name was used and how and by whom were they obtained?

- Who took the victim to get the passport/identity document photograph, and where was it taken?

- If the victim used her own genuine passport/identity document or a forged one, was an entry/exit visa required?

- If so, which embassy visa sections were visited? Did the victim go in person or was he/she accompanied, if so, by whom? What date and time was the visit made? Was any fee paid, by whom and by what means? Was a receipt issued? Were the date and time stamped? Does he/she know the identity of the visa officer that dealt with the application? Can he/she provide a description of the visa officer?

- Were any other documents used to support the visa application, such as sponsorship letters, language school registrations, employments offers, etc? If so, what were the details, and does the victim have copies?

- Where were the travel tickets purchased, and

by whom?

- By what means (cash, check or credit card) and with what name was the ticket purchased?

- What were the details of the carrier: coach, rail, ferry or airline?

- What was the date and point of departure?

- Was the victim accompanied to the port of departure? If so, how did he/she get there, and with whom?

- Did the victim travel with other victims and/or traffickers, commonly known as "mules?" If so, obtain full details.

- Who checked in with whom and at what time? What luggage was checked in? Were any purchases made at the port of departure, any duty-free purchases made on the trip, and if so, by what means and by whom?

- What seats were issued and who sat next to whom on the plane, coach, etc.?

- Were departure control checks carried out? Was the victim examined by an immigration official, border guard or customs officer before leaving? Did he/she have to complete any forms? If so, whom were they handed to?

- On entry to the transit and destination countries, did an official examine the victim, and did he/she complete any entry documentation? If so, where and when and what name did he/she give?
- Did an immigration official examine any person travelling with the victim? If so, did they complete any documentation?

Finance (Origin Locations)

- What were the financial arrangements? Did the victim pay any money in advance, or was there an agreed "debt bond" arrangement? If so, how much was the debt bond for, and how long was the victim being given to repay it?
- How were payments to be made: directly to traffickers in the country of destination or by bank or money exchange transfer to the country of origin or a third country?
- Was the victim told that he/she might have to pay additional costs in the country of destination (such as sleeping quarters, advertising or the rent of brothel premises, etc.)?

300

- How much money was promised to the victim for his/her work, and by whom?

- Was any money or other goods of value exchanged for the victim with a member of his/her family or other individual having some degree of control over him/her?

- Any information on: banks, personal or business accounts, location of the branch used in the transactions during the trafficking.

- At any stage in the recruitment and export phase, were bank cards, credit cards, traveler's checks or store charge cards used by traffickers? If so, where, when and for what purpose, i.e., to pay for the travel tickets, visa application, duty free goods, etc?

- Was foreign currency purchased prior to leaving? If so, where, when and how was it paid for?

- Did the victim ever see rental or advertising billing or phone bills? If so, how were they paid and to whom?

Transit—Transportation

Exploitation in Transit (Transit Location)

- Was the victim physically, sexually or psychologically abused during the transit phase? If so, obtain full details regarding the sexual, physical and psychological abuse.
- Was the victim unlawfully imprisoned during this period? If so, obtain full descriptions of the method and the perpetrators regarding the sexual, physical and psychological abuse.
- Did the victim come to the notice of law enforcement or other agencies while in transit?
- Was he/she stopped by the police, or did he/she seek any medical treatment or claim any state benefits while in transit? Did he/she complete any official documents for any reason? If so, obtain full details.
- Was the victim required to prostitute him/herself while in transit? If so, obtain full details of the type of prostitution, venues,

financial arrangements, etc. (see the section "Country of destination" below)

- Was the victim exploited in any other way while in transit?

- Full detailed descriptions of any additional suspects, premises and vehicles appearing in the transit phase.

- In relation to all of the above points, were there any witnesses to any of the events? If so, obtain full details.

Note: If the victim says they have been exploited consider asking further questions contained in the Destination phase and Exploitation sections.

Advertising

It is rare that advertising is found in the transit/transportation phase of trafficking in persons.

Premises (Transit Location)

- Where was the victim kept and by whom— obtain full descriptions.

- How long was the victim in the transit country and what was the nature of the conditions in which he/she was kept?
- Where did the victim visit during transit?
- Was the victim imprisoned within any transit country? Obtain full descriptions.

Communications (Transit Location)

Consider asking the questions in the origin section in the context of transit and in addition:

- Did the traffickers use new phones in transit countries? If so, does the victim now how and where they obtained them, how they paid for them and for the phone call credits?
- Did the traffickers use any other form of communication in the transit stage? If so, who did what, where and when?

Transport (Transit Location)

Consider asking the questions in the origin section in the context of transit and in addition:

- Date, location, and time of departure from the origin country, and entry into the transit country.
- What identity and/or travel documents was the victim using? Obtain full details.
- Where did the victim obtain documents?
- Were any persons travelling with the victim examined at the departure and entry points, and were any documents completed by them?
- Date, time and location of the departure point, and means of travel from the transit country
- Who was the victim with, and did departure officials examine them? If so, were any documents completed?

Finance (Transit Location)

- How were tickets/accommodations paid for?

- Who paid the money?

- Who was the money paid to?

- Where were tickets, etc., paid for?

- Who had access to money in the transit phase?

- Was any money withdrawn from banks, etc.?

- Was any money changed from one currency to another?

- Did any financial transactions take place that the victim-witness did not understand? Can they describe these?

- Who else was present when financial transactions took place?

Locations of Destination— Reception and Exploitation

Exploitation (Destination Locations)

- Was the victim allowed to keep the identity and/or travel documents upon arrival or were they taken from him/her? If so, by whom and when was this done? Where were the documents then kept?

- Was the victim unlawfully imprisoned or physically, sexually or psychologically assaulted at this initial stage? If so, obtain full details as per sexual, physical and psychological abuse.

- What form did the exploitation take: prostitution, forced labor, servitude, etc.? Was the victim engaged in prostitution?

Victims of Sexual Exploitation

- At what point did the sexual exploitation as a prostitute begin? Did the victim know that he/she was going to work as a prostitute?

- If not, at what point did the victim discover the truth and from whom?

- What type of prostitution did the victim engage in: street prostitution, off-street in apartment or house brothels, sauna or massage parlors, hostess or lap-dancing bars, or "call girl" escort agencies?

- If the victim is engaged in street prostitution: what red-light area did he/she frequent and how did he/she get there? Did a trafficker supervise him/her while he/she worked?

- Did the victim come to the notice of police or other agency? Was he/she stopped or arrested and prosecuted for soliciting? If so, when and where and what identity did he/she use?

- If the victim engaged in off-street prostitution: Where did he/she work and how did he/she get there? Who took him/her to work? Which of the traffickers were aware that he/she was working as a prostitute, and how did they know? Were they present in the brothel or on the street? Was his/her work discussed? If so, with whom?

- Was the victim supervised, and if so, by whom? What degree of liberty did he/she have?

- Could he/she leave the brothel or bar or agency unsupervised?

- Did the victim work with other prostitutes and/or maids or receptionists? If so, can he/she name and describe them?

- Was the brothel, bar or agency ever visited by law enforcement or other agency officials? If so, when, who visited, and was the victim required to give his/her name and any other particulars? If so, what name and details did he/she use?

- Whether engaged in "on or off-street" prostitution: what hours did the victim work, and what services was he/she required to provide to clients? Was he/she allowed any degree of choice as to which clients he/she entertained or which services he/she provided? Was he/she required to provide sexual services without contraceptive protection? If he/she refused, what were the consequences?

- How was the victim's ability to speak the native language? Did he/she work from a written "menu" list? If his/her language ability was limited, who translated for him/her with the clients?

Questions for Victims of other Types of Exploitation

- When did the exploitation begin?

- If the victim was to work, were working conditions different from what he/she expected?

- Was the victim living and working at the same place?

- Where did the victim work? How did he/she get there? Who took him/her there?

- Did the victim work with any other persons? Were they also victims of trafficking? Can he/she name and describe them?

- How many hours did the victim work?

- Was the victim paid, and at what rate?

- Was there a debt-bondage arrangement? If so, how much did the victim owe, and at that rate was he/she required to repay the debt? How was it paid: directly in the country of destination, or was it sent back to the country of origin? If so, by whom, and by what means, to whose account was the money credited? Were any records kept of the repayments?

- Was the victim ever hit or threatened for doing bad work or working too slowly?

- Was the victim supervised and if so, by whom; what degree of liberty did he/she have?

- Did the victim ever come to the notice of police or another agency? If so, when, where and why? What identity did he/she use?

- How was victim's ability to speak the native language?

- Was the victim required to pay additional infrastructure costs such as daily renting premises? If so, was he/she told about these additional charges before he/she left his/ her home country?

- Was the victim threatened with or subjected to violent and/or sexual abuse? Was he/she threatened with reprisals against his/her family or loved ones? Were there any other control mechanisms such as cultural or religious points of coercion?

- Were the same control mechanisms used to ensure that the victim complied with the instructions given to him/her by the traffickers?

- Was the victim threatened to be reported to authorities, resulting in deportation and/or jail?

- What was victim's general degree of liberty? Could he/she move about freely, and what was his/her state of mind? Did he/she believe that his/her traffickers would implement any of the control mechanisms outlined above?

- Was the victim allowed to communicate with family members or other workers? Was the victim allowed to make friends?

- Did the victim ask his/her trafficker if she/he could leave? Why? Why not? What happened?

- Was it possible for the victim to escape or seek assistance from law enforcement agencies? If so, did he/she attempt to do so? If not, why not? What was his/her state of mind on these points?

- Was the victim denied medical care, food, clothes or other basic necessities?

- Were others abused in front of the victim? If so, obtain full details.

- Was the victim sexually, physically or psychologically abused, or unlawfully imprisoned on any occasion? If so, obtain full details as per sexual, physical and psychological abuse.

- Obtain full descriptions as to any persons, premises and vehicles that are part of the destination country phase and that are additional to those already mentioned in the origin and transit phases.

- As a final summary, give the circumstances in which the victim is making the statement.

- Has he/she been rescued or did he/she escape by his/herself?

- In relation to all of the above points, were there any witnesses to any of the events? If so, obtain full details.

Advertising (Destination Locations)

- Does the victim know how their labor or services were advertised? In cases of sexual exploitation off-street, was it by some type of formal advertising (posters, internet, newspapers, word of mouth, etc.)

Premises (Destination Locations)

- What was the first address the victim was taken to? Who took him/her there, and how did he/she travel there?

- On arrival, were other persons/victims present? What did the premises consist of? Can he/she describe the premises in detail?

- Did the victim stay in the same premises during his/her complete stay in the destination country? Who did he/she live with? Where was the victim taken to in the destination country? Did he/she change the premises during her stay?

- Obtain full description of any premises in which the victim was required to engage in prostitution or other forms of exploitation—including detail of the layout, decoration and any other peculiarities.

- If the victim was taken to any other premises as part of the trafficking process, such as embassy visa sections, other government buildings, hospitals, clinics, language schools or other premises—obtain full details.

Communications (Destination Locations)

- Did you ever have access to a phone while you were here?
- Did you see phones being used?
- Who was using them?
- Do you know where those phones are now?
- What conversations did you over hear by people on those phones?
- Did you make calls or emails or write letters home?
- Who did you call, write to, contact?
- What did you say in those contacts home?
- If you emailed, where was the computer?
- Did other people use this computer? Who? For what reason?

Transport

At destination locations the same questions asked at the origin location should be considered and additionally:

Entry into Country:

- Date, time and location of entry point in to the country of destination.

- Was the entry covert or overt?

- If covert, what methods were used? Who was the victim with? What was the mode of transport, and was the vehicle stopped at the border crossing point? If by boat, where was the landing point, and who met him/her?

- If overt, what was the mode of transport? Did a law enforcement official at the border crossing point examine the victim? Did he/she complete any documentation such as landing cards, customs declarations, etc?

- What identity and/or travel documents was the victim using? Where are they? And what are the full details?

- Did the employer/trafficker use the victim's identity for another purpose?

- Were any persons travelling with the victim examined at the entry point and were any documents completed by them?

- Was the victim met by anybody at the entry point? If so, by whom? Obtain full description.

- At the conclusion of the shift, was the victim taken back to the "safe house" or did he/she remain in the brothel premises? If he/she went to a "safe house," how did he/she get there and who took him/her?

Finance:

- What prices did the victim charge for his/her services? Can he/she state his/her average daily earnings and estimate the total that he/she earned from prostitution during the duration of his/her exploitation? How much (if anything) was the victim allowed to keep?

- What happened to the victim's earnings? Were they handed over to a trafficker/receptionist/"maid" after each client, or did he/she hand them all over at the end of the shift? Were any records kept? Did the victim keep his/her own records?

- Did the victim buy any items for his/her exploiters with his/her prostitute earnings, such as jewelry or clothing? If so where and when, description and cost, existence and location of the items and any receipts?

- Was there a percentage split of victim's earnings between him/herself and the trafficker, or was all the money handed over? Who instructed him/her as to the scale of charges?

- Was there a debt-bond arrangement? If so, how much did the victim owe, and at what rate was he/she required to repay the debt? How was it paid: direct in the country of destination, or was it sent back to the origin country? If so, by whom and by what means? To whose account was the money credited? Were any records kept of the repayments?

- Was the victim required to pay additional infrastructure costs, such as daily renting of premises or for advertisements? If so, was he/she told about these additional charges before he/she left this/her home country?

- Was there a system of fines? If so, what how much were the fines and what were they for?

- Did the victim remit any money back home?

CHAPTER 9

LEGAL TOOLS FOR PROSECUTION

The Trafficking Victims Protection Act (TVPA) was enacted by the federal government in October 2000. Prior to its enactment, no comprehensive federal law existed to protect victims of human trafficking or to prosecute their traffickers. Congress subsequently passed the TVPA Reauthorization Acts of 2003 and 2005 (TVPRA), slightly amending the TVPA and reallocating funding to achieve the goals of the original TVPA.

The TVPA and TVPRA are comprehensive and proffer a four pronged attack on human trafficking in the U.S. First, they provide for preventative measures against trafficking of humans across U.S. borders. Second, they provide for adequate prosecution of those who traffic in human beings.

Third, they offer assistance and protection to trafficking victims already in the U.S. Fourth, they provide for the monitoring of other nations" activities that contribute to human trafficking.

Law enforcement officers are most likely to be involved with the second prong of the TVPA and TVPRA, which focuses on strengthening the ability of federal agencies to prosecute and punish traffickers. The TVPA increased mandatory minimum sentences for "peonage," "enticement into slavery," and 'sale into involuntary servitude" from 10 to 20 years in prison. The TVPA also provided for the criminal sanction of a life sentence for trafficking cases in which kidnapping, sexual abuse or killing (or any attempt thereof) occurs. Because those three criminal provisions alone were insufficient to effectively prosecute human traffickers, Congress criminalized four additional criminal acts: "forced labor," "trafficking with respect to peonage, slavery, involuntary servitude, or forced labor," 'sex trafficking of children or by force, fraud, or coercion," and "unlawful conduct with respect to documents in furtherance of trafficking, peonage, slavery, involuntary servitude, or forced labor." Additionally, Congress established a right in the victim to mandatory restitution for any of the aforementioned offenses.

The TVPA also includes traffickers" use of psychological coercion, trickery, and the seizure of documents as sufficient elements to prove trafficking has occurred. The 2003 TVPRA sought to further enhance the prosecution of trafficking-related crimes by including human trafficking under the federal Racketeering Influenced and Corrupt Organization (RICO) statute.

TVPA imposes stricter sentences on those convicted of committing crimes of human trafficking. For example, if a trafficking crime results in death or if the crime includes kidnapping, an attempted kidnapping, aggravated sexual abuse, attempted aggravated sexual abuse, or an attempt to kill, the trafficker could be sentenced to life in prison. Traffickers who exploit children (under the age of 14) using force, fraud or coercion, for the purpose of sex trafficking can be imprisoned for life. If the victim was a child between the age of 14 and 18 and the sex trafficking did not involve force, fraud or coercion, the trafficker could receive up to 20 years in prison. Moreover, the law addresses the subtle means of coercion used by traffickers to bind their victims into servitude, including: psychological coercion, trickery, and the seizure of documents, activities which were difficult to prosecute under preexisting involuntary servitude statutes and case law.

Relevant Trafficking Laws

At the federal level, numerous domestic laws might be applied to human trafficking cases. Sex trafficking was criminalized by 18 U.S.C. §1591, which makes it illegal to recruit, entice, provide, harbor, maintain, or transport a person or to benefit from involvement in causing the person to engage in a commercial sex act, knowing that force, fraud, or coercion was used or that the person was under the age of 18. Sex traffickers also may face charges under other federal statutes applicable to sex trafficking, such as 18 U.S.C. § 2423(a), prohibiting transportation of a minor with intent that the individual engage in criminal sexual activity. On the labor trafficking side, 18 U.S.C. §§1589-1590 make it illegal to knowingly provide or obtain the labor of a person by certain means, such as force or threats of force, or to traffic a person for labor or services by means of force, coercion, or fraud for the purpose of subjecting the person to slavery, involuntary servitude, debt bondage, or peonage.

Protection and assistance for victims of trafficking under the law includes legal assistance and interpretation, job training and counseling programs. The TVPA establishes a new visa status, the T visa, which allows victims of severe forms of trafficking to become temporary residents of the United States. The T visa signifies a shift in the immigration law policy, which previously treated victims of trafficking as illegal aliens subject to deportation. The T visa is a critical tool as it will help keep victims in the United States legally so they can cooperate with you and serve as witnesses for the prosecution.

The law makes victims of severe forms of trafficking eligible for benefits and services under Federal or state programs once they become certified by the U.S. Department of Health and Human Services. Once certified, trafficking victims will be eligible to apply for benefits and services under any Federal or state funded programs, to the same extent as refugees. Certified victims are also eligible for refugee cash, medical assistance and social services. Victims under 18 years of age do not need to be certified in order to be eligible for benefits and services. For these victims, the Department of Health and Human Services issues a "Letter of Eligibility" so that they have proof of eligibility for federally funded and administered benefits and services. Victims of human trafficking who are non-U.S. citizens are eligible to receive benefits and services through the TVPA to the same extent as refugees. Victims, who are U.S. citizens, do not need to be certified by HHS and are already eligible to receive many of these benefits.

A National Institute of Justice sponsored study surveyed federal and state prosecutors who had handled human trafficking cases under TVPA. The respondents identified a number of unique and potentially frustrating issues they encountered during their prosecutorial efforts. Chief among the issues the respondents encountered was an average prosecution time which could take between two to three time longer to adjudicate human trafficking cases that other federal cases. Other issues encountered by prosecutors included:

The lack of knowledge of trafficking issues among some law enforcement (federal, state, and local), prosecutors, and judges hearing cases made identifying cases, bringing them to trial, and prosecuting them difficult.

Victims returning to their trafficking situation-In some cases, because victims did not have a safe place to stay and legal means for earning money to support themselves and/or their families, they were vulnerable to re-victimization.

Ineffective communication with the victims - With language barriers and victim's unwillingness or in many cases, inability to talk about their traumatic experiences, moving cases forward for prosecution was sometimes difficult.

Lack of funding/resources - The limited availability of funding and personnel resources on the part of law enforcement to investigate cases and gather evidence and on the part of the prosecution to prepare for and prosecute cases was noted as a significant challenge. Additionally, the limitation on resources available to provide needed services to victims was also a challenge that impacted the case because unstable victims were not able to effectively contribute to the prosecution.

Recanting witnesses - Given the dependence of many of these cases on the victim's cooperation and testimony, a recanting witness often resulted in significant delays in taking a case to trial.

Lack of connection with immigrant communities - This was seen as a barrier because the lack of connections with immigrant communities specifically was attributed to one of the reasons (other than lack of funding) for why appropriate services were not readily available to victims.

Elements of a Successful Case

According to the federal prosecutors interviewed, successful cases (measured as a conviction) depend on: victim testimony; excellent agents that can develop an immediate rapport with the victims; patience with victim; trained investigators; collaborative relationships among victims, the U.S. Attorney's Office, and FBI/ICE; bridge with the NGO community; and gaining the trust of the victim. Half of the prosecutors interviewed indicated that a case is rarely successfully without victim cooperation and testimony. Once a decision is made to move forward with a case, according to prosecutors, cases rarely get dropped. In fact, 80% reported that none of their TVPA cases have resulted in dropped charges.

Fiscal year 2010 saw the greatest number of U.S. federal human trafficking prosecutions initiated in a single year. According to the 2011 *TIP Report*, "Collectively federal law enforcement charged 181 individuals, and obtained 141 convictions in 103 human trafficking prosecutions (32 labor trafficking and 71 sex trafficking)." The average prison sentence was 11.8 years, with prison terms ranging from 3 months to 54 years.

Prosecutors noted that these cases require a greater concern for victims and their needs by the prosecution than with other cases. While a challenge, this was also viewed as critical as these cases were described as victim-dependent. Other challenges that came from working with the victims included: determining who was a victim from the onset, language and cultural barriers, ability to obtain "truthful" testimony from the victims given their fear of the trafficker, lack of trust of authority figures, and the presence of extended family abroad and concerns this raised for the victims, and tactics by the defense attorneys, specifically trying to use obtainment of a visa or receiving social services as a way to discredit the victim. This was, however, identified as an unsuccessful tactic as none of the prosecutors were able to identify a case in which this tactic was successful.

The NIJ study also related some suggestions offered by other prosecutors to those who are newly assigned prosecute human trafficking cases.

- Be patient and set low expectations
- Be ready to make a significant investment of time
- Be sensitive to the victims
- Establish a good rapport with law enforcement
- Be creative with investigative techniques
- Be proactive about what charges can be brought against the defendants

Interstate Sex Trafficking

The use of the Internet gives us new tools in our efforts to investigate sex trafficking.

At the prosecution stage, a broad reading of the interstate commerce element of §1591(a)(1) allows prosecutors to bring a potentially wider range of sex trafficking cases involving online activity under federal trafficking laws, as illustrated in the recent Eleventh Circuit decision in *United States v. Timothy Myers.*

The defendants, who were charged with trafficking two girls under the age of 18 for sex, placed advertisements featuring their victims on craigslist.com and backpage.com. Testimony from Craigslist's customer service manager revealed that "the data for its websites was stored on servers in Arizona and California and that Craigslist payments end up in the company accounts in California, where the company is based.

The court concluded that the interstate commerce element of the statute was satisfied, by virtue of the movement of monies through accounts and information through servers in various states. With many social networking and online classified sites maintaining servers in multiple states, decisions such as *United States v. Myers* could allow a greater number of prosecutors to bring sex trafficking cases involving online activity in federal courts, allowing victims to benefit from the protections offered under the TVPA.

Human Trafficking Case Law Database

http://www.law.umich.edu/clinical/HuTrafficCases/Pages/searchdatabase.aspx

Training and Tools

- Local organizations specializing in working with trafficked women, including hours and procedure before making contact.
- Organizations specializing in working with trafficked women in relevant home countries
- Free health services (general practice, reproductive health, hospital and mental services, where available)
- Sources of advice on housing and other social services
- Legal aid/ immigration advice services
- Country embassies
- Shelter services
- Local churches/ community support organizations
- Language training centers
- Non-governmental organizations in the women's home country

CHAPTER 10

INTERNET INVESTIGATIONS

Internet Trends and Trafficking Online

Between 2005 and 2010, the number of Internet users worldwide reportedly doubled, passing 2 billion in 2010. In the United States, 79 percent of the population uses the Internet and almost half use at least one social networking site. Internet technologies, social networking sites, and digital networks give users the unprecedented ability to connect and communicate with individuals and large audiences over vast distances. Such technological capabilities enable traffickers by increasing their ability to exploit a greater number of victims across geographic boundaries.

Online classified websites also have seen significant growth in the number of users. Between 2007 and 2010 the number of online Americans who reported using sites such as craigslist increased from 32 percent to 53 percent. Online classified services such as craigslist operate similarly to classic "dead-tree" newspapers where individuals can posts advertisements by category such as products, services, and personals. Compared to traditional newspapers, online classified sites allow their customers to reach a wider audience and may be less expensive or even free of charge.

Traffickers have taken advantage of online classified services such as craigslist. According to Ernie Allen, president and CEO of the **National Center to Missing and Exploited Children** "Online classified ads make it possible to pimp these kids to prospective customers with little risk,"

Finding Human Sex Trafficking Online

Determining and investigating sex trafficking online poses several distinct challenges and opportunities. It is relatively easy to locate sex trafficking on a variety of internet forums including Craigslist, Backpage, Myredbook, and other membership only or specialty sites. The challenge can be differentiating the advertisements of trafficking victims versus those of sex workers who do not fall with the legal definition of trafficking. Under federal law all minors engaged in commercial sex acts are treated as victims of trafficking.

Although online classifieds commonly misrepresent the age of victims, there are certain keywords, themes, and terms designed to serve as signals to those interested in sex with a minor. While the signals and terms may change, the use of the Internet as a venue to offer those victims for sale will likely remain constant. A simple internet search shows multiple instances where suspects have been convicted of using social networking or internet classified advertisements to sexually exploit underage minors.

Even members and associates of the Gambino organized crime family have pled guilty to sex trafficking and sex trafficking of a minor after placing advertisements for their prostitution business on Craigslist and other websites.

For years Craigslist enjoyed the spotlight as the place to go to for sexual services. However, the "Adult Services" section of the site was closed in September 2010 as a result of negative publicity and intense public pressure. This caused many customers and providers to switch to other sites. In a recent statement the U.S. Attorney's Office in Atlanta stated: "The source now is Backpage, aside from underground and quasi-underground chat rooms."

However, prostitution related services never disappeared from Craigslist. They just moved from the "Adult Services" section to the "Casual Encounters," "Misc Romance," and personal advertisements.

Craigslist Investigations

Reviewing online classified ads in search of trafficking activity has been described as "challenging." It is highly likely an investigator will have to sift through hundreds of advertisements before located one related to trafficking. A common starting point for investigators is the appearance of the victim in photos used by sex traffickers to advertise. According to public records federal law enforcement agents frequently review pictures in online classified ads, noting when a girl seems younger than her advertised age. An advertisement that only shows the female's body from the neck down may also indicate that the person is underage. Agents may then undertake investigations based on a picture that appears to feature an underage girl. However, traffickers have quickly learned from this and rarely post images on the advertisements, opting to exchange photos before arranging a meeting.

According to Police Technical Instructor Wayne Nichols, a recognized expert on Craigslist investigations, knowing where to look and the words to search for are the keys to locating possible human trafficking victims on Craigslist. Locating sex trafficking on Craigslist is easy. Simply click on the "Casual Encounters" section and the "W4M" (Women for Men) area. The challenge is distinguishing those advertisements involving human trafficking from those who are voluntarily in the sex trade.

While the language may change, there are certain common phrases, key words, and codes which can narrow the search for trafficking victims on Craigslist and other internet marketplaces:

Age 17/18/19- This can sometimes be a keyword/clue indicating the victim is young without explicitly stating they are underage

Young- Another common keyword indicating the youngish appearance or age of the victim

New in town/area back in town/area - This may indicate the victim has been transported from another area.

In call/out call/hotel/host/hosting- Frequently used with prostitutes to describe whether customers come to them

Donations/roses- Some rocket scientist decided that if they used the code word roses instead of dollars and/or asked for donations that it somehow evades any prostitution related charges.   You will commonly find these on overt prostitution sites such as eros.com, backpage.com, and myredbook.com.

Dirty old men/man Seeking older man - It is not uncommon to see advertisements for "women" seeking older men. This may be a clue that the victim is younger without specifying it in the description.

Daddy/daughter incest- Creepy but self-explanatory.

Another possible indicator the victim has been trafficked is to look for out of area phone numbers. Most contact through Craigslist postings are initiated through a response to the advertisement. However, some postings, as well as postings on other sites, will list a contact phone number.

Finding suspicious language or postings

Once a suspicious posting has been identified there are several important steps to be taken. The first is to preserve the original posting either by saving the page or an electronic copy of the page. This can be as simple as printing the page to a PDF file. Craigslist only saves the most recent version of an advertisement and does not track the evolution of a particular posting.

The next step is to investigate the poster of the advertisement. Craigslist is surprisingly cooperative with law enforcement and maintains some significant information which can be useful in an investigation. However, absent exigent circumstances Craigslist will require proper legal service such as a court order, search warrant, or subpoena, before they will release any information.

Craigslist captures the internet protocol (IP) address associated with the opening and modification of a posting.

An IP address is a numerical value associated to a computer or other device. The IP address can be roughly analogized to a phone number for a particular computer and can assist with identifying which computer or mobile device posted a particular advertisement on Craigslist.

For personal advertisements, including "Casual Encounters" a verified phone number is required, which is routinely a cellular telephone. Craigslist logs every posting associated with an email address even if they are in different or unrelated categories. Craigslist records limited information on all responses to a posting such as the IP address and email address of the responder but not the actual message content.

Internet Advertisements, Sports and Human Trafficking

A number of studies have reported an increase in human trafficking during Super Bowl games. For example, during the 2009 Super Bowl, in Tampa, Florida, the Department of Children and Families took in 24 children trafficked to the city for sex. Additionally, approximately 50 girls were rescued during the previous two Super Bowl games. Internet classified ads featuring child victims of prostitution rose sharply in February 2009 in advance of the Super Bowl. *Time* reported that during Super Bowl XLIV in Miami, one man was arrested after posting an ad featuring a 14-year-old on Craigslist as a "Super Bowl special."

Super Bowl XLV, held on February 6, 2011, in Dallas, presented an opportunity to conduct new research on this subject. In anticipation of the event, Texas Attorney General Greg Abbott described the Super Bowl as "one of the biggest human trafficking events in the United States."

The University of Southern California's Annenberg Center on Communication Leadership & Policy studied the Adult section of Backpage.com for the Dallas Area, focusing on the Female Escorts section. The study revealed a noticeable spike in the number of unique posts per day on February 5 and 6. More than 300 escort ads were posted on each of these two days, compared to the overall average of 129 posts per day during the period surveyed.

Researchers conducted a content analysis of the ads searched. The word cloud below represents the most salient words extracted from posts on Super Bowl Sunday:

The bigger a word appears, the more frequently the word appears on the site. As the image shows, the most salient words are mostly related to the Super Bowl and various "specials" that were offered. Other keywords of interest that emerged include "visiting," "Iowa," "Vegas," and "Cali," which suggest that prostitutes might have traveled or been transported across state lines specifically for the Super Bowl.

In anticipations of large, highly publicized events such as the Super Bowl investigators can use the same tools as those used by the USC researchers to visualize large amounts of data.

Social Networking Sites

Beyond advertising sexual services, human traffickers also use the Internet to interact with and recruit potential victims. In four of the cases reviewed, traffickers used social media as a recruiting tool. As an example in June 2010, Dwayne Lawson was sentenced to 210 months in federal prison after pleading guilty to sex trafficking of children. The investigation began when Los Angeles police arrested a teenage girl for prostitution who was later determined to be a runaway working for Lawson. The suspect initially "contacted the girl in the fall of 2008 on Myspace.com and, after promising to make her a 'star,'" gave her a bus ticket from Florida to Las Vegas, Nevada."

Human trafficking and social networking sites are often reactive investigations undertaken in response to a runaway juvenile. An examination of the missing persons social networking activities can be helpful in identifying if the child was recruited for the purposes of sex trafficking, as well as, providing leads to his/her current whereabouts.

An estimated 41.6 percent of the U.S. population has a Facebook account and it is one of most popular social networking websites. It is through Facebook and other social networking sites that traffickers attempt to recruit their victims.

A Facebook user is able to contact other individuals by adding them to their "friends list," which enables them to be able to write on other friends" walls (i.e. a space for public commentary) and leave tags on photographs. Users are also able to communicate by sending instant messages which can sometimes be stored on the user's machine and messages, similar to emails.

The owner of the account is able to adjust privacy settings so as to restrict what information is publically accessible and what details may be viewed only by friends. Much like conventional email correspondence, sent and received messages are unable to be edited and are stored on the Facebook servers in their original format until deleted by the user of an account. Correspondence made via Facebook, including media files uploaded to the website or shared, are stored permanently on the respective account.

It is necessary for the user to manually select items of correspondence or specific files for deletion in order to have them removed from the account. Alternatively, a user may close their entire account in order to have all correspondence or media files erased. Deleted data files or accounts are no longer available to members of the public, online friends or the original account owner; however, all of this content remains archived by Facebook for a period of ninety (90) days.

Investigating Facebook

Facebook maintains a variety of data about their subscribers including:

Basic Subscriber Information

Previously referred to as "neoselect," these records will include the User Identification Number, account email address, time/date of account creation, associated telephone number(s), and time/date of logins for the past 72 hours.

Expanded Subscriber Content

Previously referred to as "neoprint," these records will include all profile contact information, status updates, files/photographs that have been shared, messages posted on other individual's walls, listings of friends and group memberships, and event reminders.

User Photographs

Previously referred to as "photoprint," this will include all photographic media uploaded by the account holder as well as photographs from third parties which have been tagged as featuring the account holder.

Messaging Correspondence

Incoming (received), outgoing (sent), and draft email equivalent communications.

Internet Logs

Commonly referred to as IP logs, this content will assist in demonstrating the time/date that a user account was accessed as well as provide enough information to trace the physical address of the computing device used to make the account access.

CHAPTER 11

TYPES OF RECOVERY/ ENFORCEMENT OPERATIONS

One of the biggest problems in conducting human trafficking investigations is locating victims. Outside of referrals through citizen's reports or from social services and non-governmental organizations, victims of human trafficking are found by law enforcement in a variety of different types of operations or by frontline law enforcement working the streets.

Many investigators would agree that educating frontline staff (patrol officers and deputies) is one of the key components of locating victims of human trafficking. There are a myriad of ways to ensure that your patrol staff learns the indicators of human trafficking and how to initiate investigations. A "Beat Officer" has a vast knowledge of the area he/she works and can provide investigators areas or locations to target operations. Providing consistent line-up/roll call trainings, pamphlets developed by any number of agencies, and including patrol staff with special operations that focus on the recovery of human trafficking victims are only a few ways to keep your frontline employees up to date on human trafficking trends and investigations.

When to initiate human trafficking enforcement operations and investigations:

There are many sources of how complaints of human trafficking come about with jurisdictions. Here are some of the ways that agencies discover human trafficking crimes and recover victims:

- Patrol / Other Non-Vice Units (Special Ops, Special Investigations, Other Investigative Units) can discover these crimes while conducting patrol activities or special enforcement (Narcotics, traffic enforcement or general criminal investigations)

- Citizen Complaints / Vice Incident Reports
  - Competitors reporting other brothels or pimps working in the area
  - Citizens reporting suspicious activity consistent to human trafficking (prostitution or brothels)
  - Other Jurisdictions (Other City Departments/ Code Enforcement)
- Apartment/Condo Management reporting brothels or underage girls or safe houses
- Self-Initiated activity by investigative units.

Patrol Initiated

- Locating runaways or arrests for street level prostitution. Often these contacts develop into discovering that the runaway or prostitute is a victim of sex trafficking.
- Locating Brothels during 911 hang-ups, citizen contacts, robberies or other non-human trafficking related calls for service at residences or apartments.

- Vehicle enforcement stops where the patrol officer discovers a car load of immigrants, or suspected prostitutes being transported.
- Locating living quarters/areas inside massage parlors or bars/cantinas.

Citizen Complaints

- Citizens reporting of houses or apartments where men are frequenting on a large scale and no women are ever seen coming and going.
- Anonymous phone calls to your agency describing young females loitering about neighborhoods or prostitution tracks.
- Citizens reporting firsthand knowledge of human trafficking activity based on their observations.

Apartment/Condo Management

Apartment and condominium staff or management can be very beneficial in initiating human trafficking investigations. Commonly, they will report what they suspect are active apartment brothels where men are commonly seen coming in and out at all hours of the day. These staff members can also provide valuable information for your investigation such as:

- Identify Address
- Possibly identify lessee
- Possible inspection of interior (layout)
- Adjacent apartments for surveillance

Self Initiated Operations

A large majority of investigations come about from self initiated activity by specialized units. There are a variety of different operations that your agency can conduct to assist in the recovery of human trafficking victims and the arrest of traffickers.

Motel/Hotel Operations

These types of operations are very common and probably the most utilized form of proactive enforcement efforts. They require a relatively large amount of planning and utilizing of experienced undercover operators. During these operations, suspected exploited children can be targeted based on intelligence from other agencies or your agency's current investigations. Mostly, the prostitutes and exploited children are discovered through internet advertisements and escort agencies.

Street Level Trolling Operations

These operations can be conducted utilizing a virtually small contingency of personnel. The operation consists of placing undercover operators in vehicles and having them drive around known prostitution tracks in an attempt to locate and arrest prostitutes. These can be excellent operations to recover exploited children and trafficked adult prostitutes. They require a minimal amount of planning and can result in great gains in the recovery of trafficking victims.

Brothel Investigations

Brothel investigations are a common type of investigation that can be conducted by law enforcement agencies. They are time consuming and very personnel intensive (surveillance and undercover operations). However, they can yield a large amount of recovered victims if coordinated properly.

Brothel investigations can consist of single-location "bust-out" operations where the investigation focuses on a single house or apartment that was discovered through investigations or complaints.

They can also become long-term enterprise/organized crime investigations that lead investigators over multi-jurisdictions and locations, with multiple suspects and victims to recover. The ladder of these two types of investigations require specialized undercover operations, intensive surveillance requirements and obtaining criminal intelligence (cell phones, financial records, identifying principal suspects and learning how the criminal organization operates).

Massage Parlor Investigations

A common retail front for human traffickers is utilizing massage parlors in their criminal enterprises. While some of these locations are legitimate massage establishments, when agencies conduct prostitution investigations, they often locate human trafficking victims working inside of these locations. The victims can be sex trafficking or labor trafficking victims or both. As in brothel investigations, these long-term investigations involving rings of massage parlors can be time and personnel intensive.

Labor Trafficking Operations

Labor Trafficking operations can be long-term investigations where you need to indentify locations, victims and suspects. Most are associated with restaurants, factories, agricultural locations and hotels.

Operational Considerations

There are a multitude of considerations to think about when conducting human trafficking operations. The following are of a few ideas to plan for when preparing for human trafficking enforcement/recovery operations:

District Attorney and United States Attorney's Office

Prior to conducting human trafficking operations, make every effort to meet with the District Attorney/United States Attorney within your jurisdiction. These meetings can prevent major legal issues in your operations and can assist with preventing redundancy and insuring that all elements of the charges you are seeking are met. In large scale operations, it is often helpful to have a District Attorney present for any legal questions if possible.

Federal Agencies and Other Law Enforcement

Federal law enforcement agencies can provide a wealth of assistance in human trafficking investigations. Consider getting these agencies involved at the beginning of your investigation and obtain valuable rapport with special agents. Federal agencies can assist with equipment, personnel and victim assistance. Many federal agents also have a variety of experience when dealing with human trafficking investigations that you can utilize to plan your operations and deal with post-operational issues.

Additionally, while conducting human trafficking investigations the possibility of federal charges might be prevalent within your case. Having an agent from a federal agency involved can prove to be essential when presenting your investigation to the United States Attorney.

Language Assistances

As previously discussed in this guide book, having qualified interpreters available at the time of your operations is essential, especially if you are expecting to recover victims who's primarily languages are not English. It is not uncommon to have multiple languages spoken by victims and suspects during a single investigation. Make sure that your investigation plan includes intelligence gathering on possible languages spoken by victims and suspects that you might encounter. Make every effort to ensure that these language specialists are sworn law enforcement - this will be beneficial during any court proceedings following your operation.

Non Governmental Organizations (NGO)/Victim Assistance

NGO's and Victim Assistance Specialists can prove to be a valuable asset in your investigations. NGO's provide assistance to victims of human trafficking by providing counseling, shelter, money and assistance with obtaining temporary immigration status (T and U Visas).

Asset Seizures

Asset forfeiture should be a part of every investigation plan/operation for human trafficking cases. Consider cash, savings/checking accounts, real estate and vehicle forfeiture when conducting operations. Often times, traffickers take great efforts to conceal their assets, so ensure that you have personnel/investigators that are current on asset forfeiture procedures and laws.

CONCLUSION

As you can see there are many complex parts to human trafficking investigations. They can be tiresome and vexing – yet very rewarding. Investigators need to be innovative and resourceful when placing all of the puzzle pieces of these cases together. As I mentioned in the introduction of this book – don't be afraid to call upon the resources of other agencies and the federal government for assistance.

Although human trafficking crimes are commonly smothered by high profile violent crimes and drug trafficking on the evening news each day; you need to understand and explain to others, that human trafficking crimes are commonly the impetus and motive behind many other crimes in our society. There have been many new advances to combat human trafficking and educating the public about this epidemic. An example of this is the recent passing of the CASE Act (Proposition 35) in California. This legislation passed by an overwhelmingly large majority of California Voters, encompasses stiffer prison terms and mandatory education for law enforcement. There are many other states looking to develop or enhance their human trafficking laws.

Challenge yourself to conduct a comprehensive and through investigation. And remember - rescuing one child, or reuniting one family, who have been subjected to the modern day slavery of a human trafficker, *can make a difference!*

Made in the USA
Coppell, TX
07 November 2021